PHILIPPIANS
Life at Its Best

PHILIPPIANS
Life at Its Best

Robert J. Dean

BROADMAN PRESS
Nashville, Tennessee

4213-77

ISBN: 0-8054-1377-4

Dewey Decimal Classification: 222.13

Subject heading: BIBLE. N.T. PHILIPPIANS

Library of Congress Catalog Number: 78-73279

Printed in the United States of America

Dedicated to
FRANK STAGG
whose teaching, writings, and spirit
make the study of the New Testament
a challenge and a pilgrimage

Preface

Have you ever noticed how many radio and television commercials use the word "life"? The advertisers know that everyone is interested in life. If advertisers can succeed in identifying their product with the good life, they have a distinct edge in the battle for consumers' pocketbooks.

Life is a key word and idea in the Bible. Physical life is a gift of God. And God wants us to know a quality of life that is life indeed, not some counterfeit version of the real thing. Jesus Christ is repeatedly described in terms of life: the bread of life; the resurrection and the life; the way, the truth, and the life. He said, "I came that they might have life, and have it abundantly" (John 10:10).

Paul's letter to the Philippians is an excellent study of the meaning of this abundant life, or life at its best. Paul's words to the Philippian Christians help us see life at its best from many perspectives. In Philippians we see what this life is and what it does. Here is the secret of a life of joy and peace—in good times and in bad. Here is a life that is not dependent on circumstances—that can face difficulties and even death with courage and hope. Here are the factors that nurture and enrich life at its best. Here are the dangers to avoid—the things that thwart and diminish the quality of life as it should be.

Philippians—Life at Its Best is an expository commentary designed to provide help in understanding the meaning and applying the message of Paul's letter. This is an ambitious task—ambitious because careful biblical interpretation is an exacting task and because applications are often either too general or too personal. However, ultimately meaning and message, interpretation and application must come together for the pastor, teacher, or individual student. Interpretation alone falls short of its purpose. Application alone can be too easily detached from the meaning of the text and thus can become speculation, opinion, and even error. Thus this expository commentary attempts to combine the two.

ROBERT J. DEAN

Contents

1

Good News Partners

Philippians 1:1-11

Suppose you are rummaging through an attic and find a faded old letter at the bottom of a trunk. It appears to have been written many years ago. You probably will read the letter, trying to find the answers to such questions as: Who wrote it? When was it written? To whom was it written? If your curiosity is sufficiently aroused, you may also try to answer this question: Why was it written? Understanding what you read in the letter depends on finding answers to some or all of these questions.

If the letter is complete and still legible, you may be able to answer the first three questions merely by reading it. On the other hand, if part of it is missing or illegible, you may have to look elsewhere. You may be able to find an envelope or some other letters in the same handwriting. The names or dates on other letters can help identify the author and approximate date of the letter in question.

The answer to why the letter was written may be apparent from the letter itself. Often, however, you will have to make an educated guess based on reading between the lines. Other letters from the same person would help. Even better would be finding a letter or letters from the person to whom the mystery letter was written. Then you would have both sides of the correspondence. Generally speaking, the more you know about the persons involved and the situation, the better able you will be to understand what you read.

We face a somewhat similar situation when we seek to understand Philippians. More than half of the books in the New Testament are ancient letters. If we want to understand what one of these letters means, we ask the same questions we would ask about the old letter in the attic.

Of course, Philippians is much older than any letter you might find in a trunk. This makes answering the questions all the more difficult. But in trying to understand it, we follow much the same process used with the letter in the trunk. We examine the letter itself for possible clues. In addition we examine other writings by the same author. And we study other records about him and the people to whom he wrote.

A Personal Greeting (1:1-2)

When we begin to read Philippians, we immediately find the answers to two of our questions. The greeting includes the name of the writer, Paul, and the name of the persons to whom he wrote— "all the saints in Christ Jesus who are at Philippi, with the bishops and deacons" (1:1).

Today you begin a letter by greeting the person you are writing, but you do not give your name until the end. However, in the first century the writer gave his own name at the very beginning. Thus Paul was following the custom of his day.

Who was Paul? Fortunately, we have more than this short letter as sources to answer this question. The New Testament contains thirteen letters whose first word is *Paul*. In addition, the book of Acts gives a wealth of information about this remarkable man. All of this external evidence about Paul is invaluable when we seek to understand this letter from Paul.

Actually the letter begins with two names—"Paul and Timothy." However, the contents show that Timothy was not a co-author. In the letter Paul used "I," not "we." In Philippians 2:19-23 he wrote of Timothy in the third person. Why then begin "Paul and Timothy"? Timothy was a trusted fellow worker, whom Paul often assigned as his representative. Paul planned to send Timothy to Philippi. Including his name in the greeting reinforced Timothy's close association with Paul.

Paul referred to himself and Timothy as "slaves." This was a familiar word in that day. It was the same word used of a person who was the property of another. Paul used the word to emphasize the nature of his relation to Christ. He was a person under divine authority. He belonged not to himself but to the Lord. His goal in life was to be an instrument of the Lord's will (see 1:19-26).

The geographic location of the recipients of Paul's letter was Philippi, a city in the Roman province of Macedonia. Ancient records shed considerable light on this ancient city. It was named for Philip II of Macedon, the father of Alexander the Great. In 42 BC the forces of Mark Antony and Octavian met and defeated the forces of Brutus and Cassius at Philippi. Antony and later Octavian settled many veterans in Philippi. They also made the city a Roman colony, a status with special prestige and privileges.

The book of Acts records a lively account of Paul's missionary work in Philippi. He went there after responding to a vision of a man of Macedonia who asked Paul for help (16:9-12). The apostle's first recorded missionary contact was at a prayer meeting on a riverbank. Presumably there was no synagogue in Philippi, only a band of devout women meeting on the sabbath for prayer. Lydia was among the converts on that day. She and her household were baptized (16:13-15).

Paul also was the instrument of help for a slave girl, who made money for her masters by her soothsaying. Her owners brought charges against Paul and Silas, his companion (16:16-19). The charges reveal a prejudice against Jews and a strong loyalty to Rome: "These men are Jews and they are disturbing our city. They advocate customs which it is not lawful for us Romans to accept or practice" (16:20-21).

Paul and Silas were beaten and imprisoned. During the night the callous Roman jailer was converted. He and his household were baptized (16:22-34). The jailer, Lydia, and possibly the slave girl became the nucleus of the Philippian church.

Paul described the congregation as "all the saints in Christ Jesus in Philippi" (Phil. 1:1). The words *in Philippi* give their geographic location, but the other words describe them in a more significant way. They were *saints* and they were *in Christ Jesus.* These are two different ways of characterizing Christians. (See 4:21 for a similar description.)

Few words have lost more of their original meaning than *saint.* The modern definition is an "especially pious and unusually good person." The New Testament word meant a person set apart by and for God. By this definition all believers are saints. A typical modern response to the word is, "I'm no saint." However, in biblical usage this would be the same as denying one's Christian faith. When Paul wrote to "all the saints . . . in Philippi," he did not have in mind a special group within a larger body of Christians (compare 4:22). He meant all the Christians, for all of them had been set apart by and for God. None of them had attained to the level of moral and spiritual excellence inherent in this experience. *Saint* Paul himself clearly denied having attained; rather he was pressing on (3:12-14).

We need this reminder in our day of watered-down moral expectations for the rank-and-file. The New Testament knows nothing of levels of dedication. There is nothing wrong with expecting much from missionaries, pastors, deacons. There is something wrong with expecting considerably less of all of us.

The words "in Christ Jesus" are even more a typical Pauline description of Christians. A generation ago James Stewart wrote his classic study of Paul, appropriately entitled *A Man in Christ.* There are two interrelated ideas in this description: (1) Each believer is personally united with Christ. This same idea is in Paul's reference to Christ being *in* a believer (Gal. 2:20). (2) All believers are bound together with Christ and with one another. This goes beyond the idea of each believer's personal relation; it includes the relation of all believers to one another in Christ. Frank Stagg points out: "Those addressed reside *in* Philippi, a city in Macedonia . . . , but their distinctive existence is *in Christ Jesus.*"[1]

"Bishops and deacons" are two categories of church leaders. The nineteenth-century English scholar J. B. Lightfoot included a study of "The Christian Ministry" in his commentary on Philippians.[2] He found that the word *bishop,* which means "overseer," was used interchangeably in the New Testament with the word "elder." Thus "bishop" in Philippians 1:1 did not refer to an ecclesiastical overseer of churches in a given area. This was a later development in church history. In Acts 20:17,28 and 1 Peter 5:1-2, two functions of elders are those of overseers and shepherds of the flock. Our word *pastor* means "shepherd." The word *deacon* means "servant." The word "deacon" is not found in Acts 6:1-7; however, the word translated "serve" is the verb form of the word translated "deacon." The qualifications for bishops and deacons are listed in 1 Timothy 3:1-13.

Paul greeted the Philippians: "Grace to you and peace from God our Father and the Lord Jesus Christ" (1:2). This greeting with minor variations is found in all Paul's letters. A greeting of some kind was a normal part of first-century letters, but the content of Paul's greeting was distinctively Christian. The typical Greek greeting was *charein* or "hail." Paul used *charis*, a cognate of *charein* that means "grace." He also used the typical Hebrew greeting "peace."

Paul's brief greeting, therefore, enables us to answer two of our questions: Who wrote the letter, and to whom was it written? Before proceeding further, there is another question that needs to be added to the list. The question may be stated in many ways. One way is, "So what?" Why all this concern with an ancient letter?

At this point the analogy between Philippians and the letter in the attic trunk breaks down. You may be interested in the attic letter only out of curiosity; or you may have some interest in the history it reveals, history perhaps of your family heritage. Philippians also has some historical interest for those who want to know more of that day and time. However, Philippians is of much more than historical value.

The letter of Paul to the Philippians is one of twenty-seven books in the New Testament. Christians consider these as inspired, authoritative records of God's unique revelation in Jesus Christ. The four Gospels record the coming, life, death, and resurrection of Jesus. The letters record the apostles' understanding and application of this unique revelation; thus they interpret the mind of Christ.

So what then? Why study Paul's letter to Philippi? We study it because it reveals the mind of Christ as interpreted by the apostle Paul. There is much more here than a letter to an ancient church and to people long since dead. Here are words of life and truth for today. The message is life at its best (see "Preface").

Some modern editions of the Greek text of the New Testament begin with a Latin quotation from a 1734 edition by J. A. Bengel. Translated it means, "Apply yourself wholly to the text; apply the whole text to yourself." Can any of us who believe in the Bible do any less?

An Expression of Gratitude (1:3-8)

Many of Paul's letters move from a brief greeting to an expression of appreciation and gratitude for those to whom he was writing. In none of his letters is the expression of gratitude more filled with warmth and joy than in the Philippian letter: "I thank my God in all my remembrance of you, always in every prayer of mine for you all making my prayer with joy" (1:3-4).

There is little doubt that Paul felt expecially close to the Philippians. He was genuinely grateful for them. Every time he thought of them he was moved to offer a prayer of gratitude and joy. He was expecially thankful for "their partnership in the gospel" (1:5). This was a partnership that had begun when they first met, and it continued at the time Paul wrote.

In fact, they had recently done something that was a key factor in why Paul wrote the letter. They had sent Epaphroditus, one of their members, with an offering to help Paul during his imprisonment. This is not spelled out until later in the letter (2:25-30; 4:18), but this was clearly in Paul's mind when he wrote this early expression of joyful gratitude.

Paul's thoughts about the Philippians called forth not only grateful joy but also confident trust. The credit for the good that had taken place among the Philippian believers belonged not to Paul, nor to the people themselves, but to the Lord. God was the one who began a good work in them, and he was the one who would "bring it to completion at the day of Jesus Christ" (1:6).

They like Paul were saints. God had called them and set them apart. The marks of their divine calling and God's continuing work of grace were already evident. However, they were pilgrims; they were on their way but not yet there. As we shall see later in the letter, the marks of their imperfection were all too evident. But Paul was confident that God had been at work among them, was still at work among them, and would continue and complete his work of grace in and through them.

The fact of Paul's "imprisonment" is mentioned in verse 7. The circumstances of this imprisonment are spelled out even more clearly in verses 12-18. This was obviously the setting for the entire letter. For this reason Philippians is generally grouped with other letters containing references to imprisonment. Ephesians, Colossians, Philemon, and Philippians are called Paul's Prison Letters.

This information speaks to one of our initial questions, When was it written? It was written during the time when Paul was a prisoner. The book of Acts tells of two long periods of imprisonment in the apostle's life. One was in Caesarea (Acts 23—26); the other was in Rome (Acts 28). Paul himself wrote of being imprisoned several times (2 Cor. 11:23). As already noted, he was briefly a prisoner in Philippi itself.

During which of these imprisonments did Paul write Philippians? The traditional site is Rome, but in more recent years Caesarea and Ephesus have also been proposed as possible places from which Paul wrote to Philippi. Advocates of Ephesus admit that the New Testament does not mention an imprisonment in that city. However, they point to Paul's passing reference to fighting wild beasts at Ephesus (1 Cor. 15:32). They believe that this tantalizing hint may refer to a period of imprisonment.

Two references in Philippians were once regarded as decisive evidence for Rome. Paul wrote of his witness among "the whole praetorian guard" (1:13), and he sent greetings from "those of Caesar's household" (4:22). Could these refer to anywhere but Rome? Study has shown that they could. The praetorian guard could refer to imperial soldiers in any imperial province, not just in Rome. Even the term "Caesar's household" could refer to emancipated imperial slaves anywhere in the Roman Empire.

Ralph P. Martin has made a thorough study of the scholarly arguments for and against each proposed location for Paul's imprisonment. He concludes: "Recent discussion of the date and origin of the letter has run into an impasse . . . . All possible identifications can present arguments that have strengths and weaknesses."[3] Fortunately, understanding Philippians does not demand that we be able to settle this issue.

Although we cannot be sure when and where Paul was in prison when he wrote Philippians, we can be sure what the Philippians did. They sent Epaphroditus, one of their own number, to Paul. He brought an offering from the Philippian church (4:18), and he himself remained with Paul to help in any way he could (2:25). This was typical of the Philippians, who at the beginning of Paul's relation with them had given financial assistance to Paul (4:15).

When we ask "Why did Paul write to the Philippians?" at least one answer is that he wrote to thank them for this expression of love. It was more than an expression of love; Paul spoke of their "partnership in the gospel." The Greek word is *koinonia*, a key New Testament concept for that which binds Christians together. The word means more than cooperation in a task. It means to have something in common, to share or to be partners.

Paul and the Philippians were partners in the gospel. They both had experienced the good news of Christ's liberation from sin and death. Paul had come to them first of all to share this good news. When they received it, they became partners, brothers with Paul in the gospel. They shared the same joyful life found in Christ, and they shared in the task of making the gospel known to others. Although Paul and most of the Philippians were many miles apart, they were bound together in their commitment to Christ's cause and in their prayerful and loving support for one another.

Verses 7-8 give further support to this idea. Paul wrote, "I hold you in my heart." Actually the Greek is ambiguous enough to be translated, "You hold me in your heart." The usual translation is the more likely meaning here. Paul expressed a similar thought in verse 8 when he said, "I yearn for you all with the affection of Christ Jesus." However, so far as the larger context is concerned, either could be the true translation because both statements are true to the facts. There was a special place in Paul's heart for the Philippians, and there was in their hearts a special place for the apostle.

Paul wrote, "You are all partakers with me of grace" (1:7). The word "partakers" translates a Greek word that describes those who share and express *koinonia.* A prefix meaning "together with" adds further emphasis to the corporate meaning of this relationship. These partners in the gospel partook together of the same grace. They were bound together by their common experience of the saving and sustaining grace of God. As Paul endured imprisonment, he was sustained by the same grace that was sufficient in every situation (2 Cor. 12:9). The Philippians also faced tests of their own; and in these they, like Paul, found the same source of strength.

Paul at times used "grace" to describe not only God's saving and sustaining grace but also believers' actions that reflected the same generous and gracious spirit. For example, he wrote to the Corinthians of the grace of God experienced and expressed by the Macedonian Christians in their liberal contributions to the offering for the poor at Jerusalem. He did so in the context of challenging the Corinthians to do their part in this same grace (2 Cor. 8:1-7).

Thus Paul probably had in mind in Philippians 1:7 their gracious response to his situation. They had sent money and one of their own members to help. Thus they shared with Paul in all that he was doing to further the cause of Christ and his good news. Particularly they shared with Paul in his immediate situation. His goal as a prisoner was not personal safety but faithfully defending and declaring the gospel (see also 1:12-20).

At the urging of William Carey the first missionary society in modern times was begun in 1792. His friend Andrew Fuller was made secretary of the newly-formed organization. They turned their attention to deciding where to begin their missionary work. A report of conditions in India stirred their hearts. Then the question arose,

Who would go as a missionary? Andrew Fuller told the group that India was like a gold mine of missionary opportunity, but that this mine was as deep as the center of the earth. "Who will venture to explore it?" Fuller asked.

Carey was quick to reply, "I will venture to go down, but remember that you—you who remain at home—must hold the ropes." Thus they entered into a covenant to be partners in the gospel. The missionary society would share in the missionary work of Carey through their prayers and financial support.

A pastor and congregation are partners in the gospel. Paul had a pastoral-type relation with the Philippian church. Although the apostle did not remain in Philippi as a resident shepherd of this flock, he had many of the ties with them that a pastor has with a congregation.

This is a unique relationship. The ties that bind pastor and people are the strongest of ties: They share together in the most decisive moments of life—the spiritual birth of new converts, the joining of two lives in marriage, the birth of children. They walk side by side through that mixture of joys and sorrows which is the Christian pilgrimage. They worship together, pray together, rejoice together, work together, weep together. Pastor and congregation help one another in their common ministry of sharing the good news of Christ. They support one another as they draw from a common source of strength—the grace of God.

An Earnest Prayer (1:9-11)

Prayer for one another is one of the ties that bind those who are good news partners. Paul's letters are filled with prayers for the churches and with requests for their prayers. He obviously believed that God can and does use intercessory prayers as channels of grace and power. There is no doubt in Paul's case that his prayers testify (1) to his awareness that the gospel is God's work and (2) to his deep and continuing concern for the churches.

The content of his prayer for the Philippians is twofold: He prayed for growing love and for increasing fruits of righteousness.

He wrote, "It is my prayer that your love may abound more and

more" (1:9). Jesus taught that love is the heart of a right relation
with God and others. He taught his followers to love God supremely
and to love one another with unselfish devotion. Paul's letters build
on and further interpret and apply this concept. Paul also prayed
that love would be combined with moral discernment and
commitment. He prayed that the Philippians might "approve what
is excellent, . . . be pure and blameless for the day of Christ, filled
with the fruits of righteousness which come through Jesus Christ to
the glory and praise of God" (1:10-11).

The word "approve" was used to describe coins that were tested
and proved to be genuine, not counterfeit. Paul wanted the
Philippians to exercise careful discernment in their attitudes and
actions. Moral integrity is easily compromised. Paul prayed that God
would help them distinguish not only good from evil but also good
from various shades of grey.

He wanted them to be filled with fruits of righteousness. Probably
he meant those qualities he elsewhere called "fruit of the Spirit"
(Gal. 5:22-23), of which love was the first on the list.

On the surface, Paul's prayer is simply a prayer for a group of
Christians to grow in love for one another and in moral discernment
and commitment. Such a prayer would be appropriate for any
group of Christians. However, in light of the entire letter, Paul
apparently felt that these areas were targeted for specific needs in
the Philippian church.

This brings us back to the question "Why did Paul write the letter
to the Philippians?" For the answer to this crucial question we must
search the letter itself for clues.

Some of the reasons for his letter are clear. As we have seen, the
Philippians had sent money and one of their number to help Paul.
Therefore, Paul wrote to express his gratitude. Yet Paul did not spell
out his thanks until the end of the letter; and even then the tone of
his expressed gratitude goes much deeper than a thank-you note.
This at least suggests that although expressing thanks for their help
was one occasion for the letter, Paul also had other purposes in
mind.

One other purpose was to report on his own situation and on the condition of Epaphroditus. The messenger from Philippi had been seriously ill, and the Philippians had heard about the illness. Therefore, Paul wrote to inform them that Epaphroditus was now well and to explain why he was sending him home (2:25-30). He also wrote to give them an update on his own situation in prison (1:12-26). Yet the manner of Paul's report suggests that he had a more serious purpose in mind.

What needs in the Philippian church was Paul trying to address in his letter? Some Bible students profess to see no real problems in the Philippian church. They feel that Paul was merely rejoicing in them and in their Christian commitment.

There is no question that joy is a theme of the letter. The words "joy" (1:4,25; 2:29; 4:1) and "rejoice" (1:18,19; 2:17,18,28; 3:1; 4:4,10) recur throughout. Much of this joy grew out of Paul's joyful gratitude for what God had done and was doing among the Philippian Christians.

Yet this note of joy is set in a context of concern about some specific needs in the church. For example, Paul called them his "joy and crown"; yet he exhorted them to "stand firm . . . in the Lord" (4:1). And in the next sentence Paul exhorted two women by name "to agree in the Lord" (4:2). This probably was not just a mild disagreement that Paul intended to touch in a light and almost humorous way. Paul asked someone he called "true yokefellow" to help these women who had labored side by side with Paul and others (4:3). Paul was concerned that they were not now laboring side by side but involved in some disagreement. Another explicit reference to this spirit is in 2:14: "Do all things without grumbling and questioning."

These brief references may seem inadequate evidence to conclude that there was any dissension in Philippi. However, Paul directed strong warnings against selfishness and pride, the hallmarks of dissension. And the key exhortations of the book are to unselfish commitment and oneness of spirit in the Lord (1:27 to 2:4). Even Paul's report on Epaphroditus' condition is part of a passage that calls for sacrificial self-giving for the cause of Christ. Paul pointed to

Christ himself as the perfect embodiment of such self-giving love (2:5-11). Then he cited himself (2:17-18), Timothy (2:19-24), and Epaphroditus (2:25-30) as three who sought to put the larger cause before their own interests and needs.

And in a passage where Paul dealt with the dangers from external opponents and persecutors, Paul made it plain that they posed no real threat to a congregation united in the Lord. External opposition can be faced victoriously so long as the Philippians "stand firm in one spirit, with one mind striving side by side for the faith of the gospel" (1:27).

The words "one," "all," and "together" are frequent in the letter, and not by accident if this analysis is correct. Notice even in 1:1-11 the repetition of "all" in verses 1,4,7,8. In verses 4,7, and 8 when Paul wrote "you all," he did not merely use the second person plural pronoun. Instead he used the word "all" with the pronoun to give emphasis to the all-inclusiveness of the plural. Given the rest of the letter, this was probably intentional and significant.

The problem of dissension in Philippi probably had not reached the proportions of what Paul had encountered in Corinth. Paul's Corinthian letters reveal the trauma of that bleak experience. The apostle was determined that he would do everything possible to spare his beloved Philippians from such pain and distress. Therefore, he responded strongly and quickly to news from Philippi that indicated a movement toward disruptive dissension.

In this light the prayer in 1:9 was an earnest petition. The best antidote for a spirit of selfishness and dissension is genuine Christian love.

We will be confronting this theme throughout Philippians, but two relevant insights are appropriate in connection with these comments on 1:1-11: (1) Partners in the gospel cannot hope to reach outsiders effectively so long as the partners are constantly at each other's throats. Nothing so contradicts the spirit of Christ as a congregation of professed Christians who are proud and contentious. On the other hand, nothing so magnifies Christ as a spirit of mutual love and concern in a church. (2) Those who care about the gospel must work fervently for a spirit of *koinonia* among the good news partners. Peacemaking is a hazardous venture. Paul knew this from personal experience. Yet he could not stand idly by while his beloved Philippians started down the road toward disunity. Because he cared, he acted to do what he could. He wrote from prison to exhort them to be one in the Lord.

In addition to incipient dissension in Philippi, the letter also reflects some moral confusion. Probably the two were interrelated.

The most explicit passages about moral confusion are in Philippians 3. Early in the chapter Paul warned of "the dogs . . . the evil-workers . . . who mutilate the flesh" (3:2). In verses 18-19 he used equally strong language to warn the congregation of those who "live as enemies of the cross." Of them he wrote, "Their end is destruction, their god is the belly, and they glory in their shame, with minds set on earthly things."

Various attempts have been made to identify these two groups and to discover the nature of their threat to the Philippians. Those mentioned in 3:2 probably were similar to those who undercut Paul's work elsewhere by insisting that circumcision was essential—if not for salvation then for acceptance into the full privileges of being among God's people (compare Acts 15:1; Gal. 1:6-7; 2:11-14). Those mentioned in Philippians 3:18-19 were probably libertines influenced by Gnostic-like teachings; on the one hand, they professed a kind of superior spirituality, but on the other hand, they saw no evil in what to Paul were obviously immoral actions.

Whatever the exact identity of these false teachers, the Philippian letter hints at some degree of moral confusion in the church. Judging from what Paul wrote in chapter 3, part of the confusion revolved around the idea of perfection. This perfectionism may have been based on pride in legalistic rituals (3:2), or in a supposed deeper level of spirituality (3:18-19), or both.

Paul went out of his way to emphasize here and elsewhere in Philippians that the Christian life is a pilgrimage. He insisted that he had not arrived at perfection (3:12-14), nor had any of those who are truly mature (3:15). The attainment of true moral maturity is still a goal, a part of the confident hope of those who live in light of Christ's coming (3:20-21). This eschatological (future) dimension is present throughout the letter (1:6,10; 2:16; 4:10-11). Notice that two of these references are in 1:1-11.

Thus when Paul prayed for the Philippians to grow in moral discernment, to choose the best, and to be filled with fruits of righteousness, the apostle probably had a specific need in mind. He was seeking to counteract the moral confusion in Philippi. Very likely this moral confusion was linked closely with the problem of disruptive dissension. The two often go together.

Paul obviously cared deeply for the Philippians. Because he cared, he wrote them . . . prayed for them . . . and intended to visit them as soon as he could (2:24). He loved the Philippians as a parent loves his child. A parent is concerned about any threat to the welfare of his child and is willing to do what he can to avert that threat. Paul knew the risks of concern, but he was willing to take risks because he cared.

Galatians 6:1 is Paul's clearest statement of the Christian's responsibility to try to help those who have gone astray. Most of the Philippians had not yet gone astray, but Paul felt some of them stood at a moral crossroads and were leaning in the wrong direction. Ordinarily most of us are leery of getting involved either with persons who have gone astray or with persons who are leaning in that direction. Time and energy—emotional as well as physical—are inevitable costs of this kind of involvement. There is no promise of success; rather there is the very real possibility of being rejected, misunderstood, and criticized—both by the persons we want to help and by many others.

Paul knew the costs and risks of involvement, but his position was that he already was involved. He was involved as a partner in the gospel with the Philippians. They were like family to him. He could no more ignore what threatened them than a person can ignore what threatens those who are closest kin to him. Because he cared, he prayed and he acted. His letter to Philippi is evidence of his concern in action.

2

Ready to Live . . . Ready to Die

Philippians 1:12-26

"Is That All There Is?" is the title of a song that was popular a few years ago. The lyrics describe a person's disillusionment with life. The singer tells of a series of experiences—all the way from going to a circus as a child to falling in love as a youth. But after each experience the singer asks "Is that all there is?" The cynical conclusion of the song seems to be that since life is short and empty, the best a person can do is to "break out the booze and have a ball."[1]

Unfortunately the song expresses the way many people feel about life. Shakespeare's Macbeth spoke for many in every generation when he defined life as "a tale that is told, full of sound and fury, signifying nothing."

Nothing could be farther from the Christian view of life. Nowhere is the Christian philosophy of life better stated than by Paul in Philippians 1:12-26. Two distinctive characteristics of the Christian view are illustrated in what the apostle wrote to the Philippians. First of all, life's circumstances do not determine the quality of life for believers. God, not circumstances, is in control; God is able to work out his good purpose even in the midst of evil circumstances (vv. 12-18). Therefore, *Christians are ready to live no matter what life brings.* Second, Christians are *ready to die no matter when death comes.* They are able to live with purpose and confidence because they have placed themselves in the hands of the one who is Lord of life and death. Christians can affirm both life and death because they know Christ who holds the keys to abundant living and eternal life (vv. 19-26).

What a contrast to the many people who are controlled by life's circumstances, devastated by trouble, fearful of death, and bored with life! Philippians 1:12-26 is without doubt a passage with a message for today.

Ready to Live—No Matter What Life Brings (1:12-18)

One of Paul's purposes for writing was to inform the Philippians of his own situation. They knew he was a prisoner. They had sent money and one of their own members to help him. Paul knew they were concerned about him, so he wanted to give them his own account of his life in prison.

Verse 12 states the heart of his report: "I want you to know, brethren, that what has happened to me has really served to advance the gospel." The word translated "really" can mean either "more" (to a greater extent) or "rather." Probably Paul intended to imply that the effect of imprisonment on the gospel had turned out differently than had been expected by some. *The New English Bible* translates verse 12: "Friends, I want you to understand that the work of the Gospel has been helped on, rather than hindered, by this business of mine."[2]

Paul did not go into a detailed description of his circumstances. That he was a prisoner is certain; where and under what conditions he was a prisoner are uncertain. The traditional view is that he was a prisoner in Rome under the circumstances described in Acts 28. This chapter depicts Paul as confined under house arrest (v. 23) awaiting his hearing before the emperor. Visitors were allowed to come to Paul; and in this context he "welcomed all who came to him, preaching the kingdom of God and teaching about the Lord Jesus Christ quite openly and unhindered" (Acts 28:30-31). Acts 28 also refers to Paul being bound with a chain (v. 20). Roman custom seems to have required that a prisoner like Paul would be chained day and night to a soldier.

All in all, the situation described in Acts 28 is not as bad as it could have been for a prisoner. For example, Paul was not treated nearly so badly as he had been during his first visit to Philippi, where he had been beaten and placed in stocks in the inner prison (Acts 16:23-24). Doubtlessly Paul's status as a Roman citizen was a factor in how he was treated during his Roman imprisonment. The local politicians in Philippi had been horrified when they discovered that they had treated a Roman citizen in such a brutal way (Acts 16:37-39). In Jerusalem a Roman tribune had ordered Paul tied up and beaten; however, when he discovered that Paul was a Roman citizen, he treated Paul very differently (Acts 22:23-29).

Yet even if we assume the best about Paul's imprisonment, it must have been a trying experience. A forced confinement of any kind is frustrating, especially for an active go-getter and traveler like Paul. Even if visitors could come and go, his own freedom of movement was gone. He may have occasionally been able to leave the house under guard; but others, not he, controlled his freedom of movement. A house is not a dungeon, but it can be just as confining.

There was also the natural anxiety about the ultimate outcome of his imprisonment. Paul knew that life and death were the issues at stake; and although he hoped for release, the outcome was by no means certain during much of the time of his confinement (see comments on Phil. 1:19-26).

Also there was the matter of being chained to a Roman soldier. If Paul as a prisoner was always chained to a soldier, he was robbed not only of freedom of movement but also of privacy. And if any of the soldiers were cruel or evil men, such an arrangement became even worse. The book of Acts tells of the consideration with which the centurion Julius treated Paul on their journey to Rome (Acts 27). Very likely, Paul was not always so fortunate, especially if he was chained over a period of time to a large number of guards.

Paul's statement in Philippians 1:13 has a strong bearing on trying to reconstruct the circumstances of his imprisonment. He claimed in verse 12 that his confinement had advanced the gospel. Verse 13 gives one of the reasons for this claim.

What was the "praetorian guard"? This translates one word in Greek, and it is debatable whether it means the praetorium (a place) or the praetorian guard. As a place, it originally meant the tent of the general of a Roman army. It had come to be used as the palace of the emperor or of a governor. The word was used like this at times in the New Testament (Matt. 27:27; Mark 15:16; John 18:28,33; 19:9; Acts 23:35).

Some translators and commentators, therefore, have assumed that Paul was referring to his faith being reported throughout the imperial palace. However, J. B. Lightfoot argued, and many others have agreed, that the common use of the term in the first century was not to the imperial palace but to the imperial guards.

Several thousand elite soldiers were attached directly to the emperor. They received higher pay and attained greater prestige than other soldiers. They had become a potent political force by the time of Paul. Not many years earlier the praetorian guard had taken charge after the assassination of Caligula. They thwarted the hopes of those who wanted to restore the Republic, and they single-handedly made Claudius the new emperor.

They were hardened veterans who could be brutal when the occasion called for it. And Paul very likely was chained day and night to one of these guards.

Paul's claim in verse 13 implies that over a period of time he had contact with a large number of these men. Otherwise, how could news of his Christian faith spread throughout the whole praetorian guard? The apostle was not claiming that he had had personal contact with every one of the thousands of guards. Rather he said they all had become aware that his imprisonment was "for Christ."

This means that Paul had chosen not to let his bad situation get him down. His confinement under trying conditions could have filled him with discouragement and self-pity. Instead Paul saw in his bleak surroundings an amazing opportunity for witness. Under what other conditions could he have had long periods of uninterrupted time with so many members of the imperial guard? Paul's best chance for an open-minded hearing of the gospel by these hardened soldiers was in the solitude of a one-to-one relationship. Had he tried to preach to a group of soldiers, they may have felt it necessary to act unconcerned; or even to ridicule Paul and his message. Not so in the quietness of Paul's room. Many of them probably still acted unconcerned, even when alone! And many probably also ridiculed the apostle. But others must have listened with much interest. And all had the rare opportunity of being with a genuine Christian and of hearing his testimony.

Paul includes in verse 13 not only the praetorian guard but also "the rest." These were those other than the soldiers who heard of Paul's faith in Christ. From Acts 28:17 we know that some in Rome heard the apostle's witness from Paul himself.

Paul did not claim that all of these people became Christians. His only claim in verse 13 is that many became aware that Paul was no criminal but a man imprisoned because of his faith in Christ. Verses 13 and 14 indicate how this happened—through Paul's own witness and also through the bold witness of other believers. There was an obvious connection between the two—Paul's boldness and theirs. In fact, this is Paul's point in verse 14: another good thing that had come as a result of his imprisonment was the bold witness of the Christian brothers in the area. "Most of the brethren have been made confident in the Lord because of my imprisonment, and are much more bold to speak the word of God without fear."

Paul's words show that there were other believers in the area. And the combined bold witness of Paul and many of these doubtlessly won some converts—both among the soldiers and "the rest."

At the end of his letter to Philippi Paul wrote, "All the saints greet you, especially those of Caesar's household" (4:22). At one time it was thought that this meant that some of the emperor's own family had been converted. But the word "household" referred to all the persons associated with the imperial palace. This would include servants of all kinds—slaves, freedmen, and possibly some of higher rank who served on the residential staff. Some of these were the bold witnesses mentioned in Philippians 1:14, but others may have been new converts who were won by the bold witness of Paul and the others.

Verses 15-17 describe another aspect of what made Paul's situation a potentially trying situation: "Some indeed preach Christ from envy and rivalry, but others from good will. The latter do it out of love, knowing that I am put here for the defense of the gospel; the former proclaim Christ out of partisanship, not sincerely but thinking to afflict me in my imprisonment." Two questions confront the interpreter: Who were these people who preached Christ from envy and rivalry? And how did they think their preaching of Christ would afflict Paul?

Some commentators have identified these as false teachers similar to those condemned in Galatians 1:6-9 and alluded to in Philippians 3:2. According to this view, these Judaizers hoped to afflict Paul by proselyting his converts while Paul was helplessly imprisoned.

Others see these as preachers of a message with strong political overtones. They hoped their revolutionary gospel would get Paul into further trouble with the political establishment.

Still other commentators identify the preachers in verse 15a as former leaders in the local church who were jealous of Paul's popularity among the believers. According to this view, they assumed that Paul would be upset if their preaching won more converts than his.

The first of these views is doubtful. Paul had nothing good to say about the false teachers in Galatians. He probably would not refer to such men as proclaiming Christ, as he does in Philippians 1:15-17. In Galatians he called in question the *message* itself; in Philippians he called in question the *motives* of the preachers, but not their message. They were preaching Christ, but they were preaching Christ for the wrong reasons.

The third view fits many of the known facts about the situation. It also fits the realities of human nature and church history. Some former leaders could have envied Paul's new popularity and resented the attention others paid him, even when he was a prisoner. Such blind envy also is just blind enough to assume that Paul would be hurt by their success just as they had been hurt by his. So they became flaming evangels in a futile attempt to cause Paul grief.

Such distorted motives no doubt did bother Paul, but he found cause to rejoice in the very thing that they had expected to bother him—their zealous proclaiming of Christ. "Whether in pretense or in truth, Christ is proclaimed; and in that I rejoice" (1:18).

Verses 15-18 hold three clear lessons. First of all, Christ can be preached by people who are moved by the wrong motives. God can use such preaching of Christ to win people to faith in Christ. Of course, he does it not because of the preachers but in spite of them.

This is both encouraging and challenging. Our motives are often mixed at best. We are not always moved most powerfully by the highest and most unselfish motives. It is encouraging to know that God can use us, when he must, in spite of ourselves.

The challenge is that we strive toward purer motives. Doing the right thing for whatever reason is better than leaving the good undone, and it is surely better than doing the wrong thing (cf. Matt. 6:1-18). However, the person who acts with selfish motives misses the highest blessings of being a channel of blessings. He also spreads his selfish and envious spirit among others. God may win a person to Christ through a preacher with selfish motives, but the new convert can become disheartened if he discovers the kind of person the preacher really is.

The second lesson is the importance of humility in Christian living and serving. This is a point to which Paul returned with great force in the heart of the letter, 1:27 to 2:30. Christians are not to act out of selfish ambition but out of unselfish commitment. Christians should be more concerned about honoring Christ than they are about how this affects them. They seek to honor Christ, and they rejoice in all those who honor Christ—even those with whom they may not agree at every point and with whom they may have personality conflicts.

The overriding lesson in verses 15-18 is the same one in verses 13-14—God can bring good out of a bad situation. Paul's classic statement of this principle is in Romans 8:28, but nowhere is that principle better illustrated than in Philippians 1:12-18. Paul did not believe that everything that happened to him was good. Much that happened was bad and painful and evil. But what Paul did believe was that "in everything God works for good with those who love him, who are called according to his purpose" (Rom. 8:28). God has a good purpose; and God sometimes uses even the bad that happens to work out his good purpose.

From our perspective we must add to Paul's list of the good that came out of his imprisonment. In the long run the Philippian letter and Paul's other Prison Letters may be the best results of his evil situation. Paul refused to let the trial of his imprisonment break his spirit. To the contrary, he availed himself of every opportunity to nourish and to share his faith in Christ.

Three centuries ago a Baptist preacher was imprisoned for preaching the gospel as he believed it. John Bunyan spent twelve long years in jail in his native England. But it was while he was a prisoner that Bunyan wrote *The Pilgrim's Progress.* Those were dark and difficult years for Bunyan, but their evil did not destroy him. To the contrary, God brought lasting good out of an evil situation. How much poorer would the world be without Bunyan's classic allegory of Christian's pilgrimage from the City of Destruction to the Celestial City?

Dietrich Bonhoeffer was imprisoned in his native Germany by the Nazis. His imprisonment and eventual martyrdom at their hands is one of the twentieth century's glowing stories of good out of an evil situation. Bonhoeffer's *Letters and Papers from Prison,* which were published after his death, have instructed and challenged our generation.

Bonhoeffer and Bunyan were Christians who like Paul showed that God not only can sustain his people in bad situations but also can actually bring some good out of such evil circumstances.

Ready for Death—No Matter When Death Comes (I:19-26)

One of the most paradoxical Christian teachings is this: Christians can rejoice in the midst of any set of circumstances. James taught this (Jas. 1:2-4,12). So did Peter (1 Pet. 1:3-8). Paul's letters are filled with this teaching (Rom. 5:1-5; 1 Thess. 5:16), with the entire Philippian letter bearing testimony to this truth. But the teaching was not original with the apostles. They were only echoing the teachings of Jesus. The Beatitudes in Matthew 5:3-12 are the classic statement of this strange but wonderful truth.

This theme, which runs through Philippians, surfaces explicitly at several points. Philippians 1:18-19 is one of those points. Paul was rejoicing in the preaching of the gospel, even though the circumstances were far from ideal. Then looking to the future he wrote, "Yes, and I shall rejoice." He rejoiced in the present, and he was confident that he would rejoice in the future.

What was the basis for this amazing confidence? Notice the rest of verse 19: "For I know that through your prayers and the help of the Spirit of Jesus Christ this will turn out for my deliverance." What did Paul mean by "my deliverance"? Was he talking about expecting to be delivered from prison? Or was it something else?

Some commentators believe Paul's primary reference was to his hope of a favorable outcome to his case and his release from imprisonment. They point to 1:25 and 2:24 as evidence that Paul was expecting to be released. These verses sound hopeful, even confident, especially 1:25. However, there are other verses that seem to indicate that Paul was facing the possibility of continued imprisonment and eventual execution (1:20; 2:17). Throughout 1:21-26 he balanced the two possibilities over against one another. Although at times he seemed to see the scales weighed in the direction of release, he also saw death as a possibility.

In any case, Paul's confident hope was not based on assurance of deliverance from prison and execution. Later in his life, when he sensed that the end was near, his confidence was unabated (2 Tim. 4:6-8). Thus when the words "my deliverance" are viewed in context, Paul was referring to the Lord's sustaining power in his life no matter what came—whether in living or dying.

Paul was completely confident of the Lord's power to keep him in life and in death. His only concern was that he would be faithful to the Lord, no matter what: "It is my eager expectation and hope that I shall not be at all ashamed, but that with full courage now as always Christ will be honored in my body, whether by life or by death" (1:20).

What an amazing statement! Paul was not fearful or anxious about those things that concern most people; his consuming concern was one that most people give little or no attention to. The fears and anxieties of humanity are legion. People fret about money, possessions, success, prestige; they fear poverty, sickness, failure, pain, death. Paul fretted about none of these goals, nor did he fear any of these terrors. His overriding concern was to be a faithful and bold witness for Christ no matter what the circumstances. What anxiety he had about the hard realities of living and dying were focused on one goal—that he be able to honor Christ, whatever his circumstances.

Paul did not expect that he would fail Christ; rather his "earnest expectation and hope" was that he would magnify Christ. The basis for Paul's hope, however, was not in himself but in the Lord.

This is the point of the words "through your prayers and the help of the Spirit of Jesus Christ" (1:19). Paul expected them to pray for something much more significant than his release from prison. In another letter from prison Paul asked his readers to pray "that utterance may be given me in opening my mouth boldly to proclaim the mystery of the gospel" (Eph. 6:19). He expected them to pray for him, and he expected God to answer their prayers. Through their prayers the empowering help of the Spirit of Jesus Christ would work in and through him. Jesus had promised his followers that his Spirit would help them witness boldly in times of trial (Luke 12:11-12). Paul claimed that promise. Later in Philippians he summed up his approach to life: "I can do all things in him who strengthens me" (4:13).

Philippians 1:21 is an equally succinct and memorable statement of the Christian view of life and death: "For to me to live is Christ, and to die is gain." His life was centered in Christ. He viewed all things from this perspective. His life was walking with and serving Christ.

The consuming passion of a person is the essential factor in what a person becomes. Jesus warned that "a man's life does not consist in the abundance of his possessions" (Luke 12:15). Yet many people confuse life with possessions. They would say, "For to me to live is making a living for myself and my family," or "For to me to live is assuring the good life by seeking financial security and success."

Others would build their lives around pleasure. "For to me to live is having a good time . . . enjoying the good things of life." Such goals determine a person's values, priorities, attitudes, and actions.

By contrast Paul wrote, "For to me to live is Christ." This commitment determined Paul's values, priorities, attitudes, and actions.

An inseparable part of this for Paul was his words "to die is gain." It was precisely because he could say "to live is Christ" that he also could say "to die is gain."

Paul was no philosopher who had reasoned his way to a belief in life after death. He was a man of faith who believed that God in Christ had conquered sin and death and made available the fruits of that victory to those who would receive them. To the Corinthians he wrote: "The sting of death is sin, and the power of sin is the law. But thanks be to God, who gives us the victory through our Lord Jesus Christ" (1 Cor. 15:56-57). Paul was already spiritually alive in Christ; he did not expect death to disrupt that relationship, only to open new dimensions of it.

Verses 22-24 explain why Paul referred to death as "gain": "If it is to be life in the flesh, that means fruitful labor for me. Yet which I shall choose I cannot tell. I am hard pressed between the two. My desire is to depart and be with Christ, for that is far better. But to remain in the flesh is more necessary on your account."

The apostle was weighing the two possibilities before him. On one hand he might be released; if so, he could continue to serve God by working with people like the Philippians. This was a satisfying and fruitful life and work. On the other hand, he might remain in prison and eventually lose his life. But this held no terrors for Paul. To the contrary, his own personal preference lay in this direction; for dying meant departing to be with Christ.

The word translated "depart" was sometimes used to speak of breaking camp and sometimes of loosing a ship from its moorings. Both analogies are graphic symbols of the Christian view of death and dying.

Death is like breaking camp. Campers loosen the tent poles, pull up the tent pegs, pack their equipment, and depart. The last words of Robert E. Lee were, "Strike the tent." The old soldier was breaking camp here and marching toward a destination beyond this life.

During the Battle of Britain when R.A.F. pilots literally saved their islands with great valor, many young men gave their lives. It was customary for their companions to speak of the dead as having been "posted to another station."

The other analogy is a ship being loosed from its moorings and setting sail. For a while it is visible as it moves out of the harbor, eventually becoming only a speck on the horizon. Then it is gone. The place at the moorings is empty, and the vessel is out of sight. In this sense it is indeed gone; but to those beyond the horizon the ship is not gone at all—it has come.

When death claims a loved one, we say, "he's gone"; but someone beyond death's horizon says, "he's here."

What is beyond that horizon? Paul does not paint details of the afterlife. Rather he says that we depart to "be with Christ." Paul repeatedly spoke of his life as "in Christ." Here he referred to the state beyond earthly life as "with Christ." The parallel is Jesus' promise to the penitent thief: "Today you will be *with me* in Paradise" (Luke 23:43).

But what about the future resurrection? How can we reconcile Philippians 1:23 with passages like 1 Thessalonians 4:13-17? One set of verses refers to going to be with Christ at death; another set speaks of a resurrection at Christ's coming, when those who have fallen asleep in Christ shall be raised.

Some people see these teachings as hopelessly contradictory. Others avoid the problem by ignoring one or the other set of verses. Still others seek a solution that takes seriously both sets of verses. The latter group generally accepts one of the following interpretations:

1. Time is not a factor beyond death. It is a different realm. From our time-bound limitations, therefore, what seems a problem is actually not a problem at all. Emil Brunner wrote: "The date of

death differs for each man, for the day of death belongs to this world. Our day of resurrection is the same for all and yet is not separated from the day of death by intervals of centuries—for these time-intervals are here, not there in the presence of God, where 'a thousand years are as a day.' "[3]

2. At death a person in Christ goes to be with Christ; however, there yet remains something more for those with Christ. Like the living they look for God's consummation when all God's people will share in the fulfillment of God's redemptive purpose. Oscar Cullmann wrote: "Hence *the dead likewise live in a condition in which the tension between present and future still exists.*"[4]

This analogy has helped me try to conceive of this: "Suppose your family has agreed to meet at a certain time and place for a reunion. Suppose you arrive at the scheduled place before the entire family has gathered. You are already there, but the reunion cannot really begin until all the family is there. Likewise the dead in Christ are already with the Lord. Their fellowship with him is already rich and wonderful. However, even they await the final resurrection when we all will be clothed with the fullness God has prepared for his own."[5]

What more can be said about the state of the dead in Christ during this period? All we know for sure, probably all we shall ever know this side of death, and all we really need to know is this: the dead in Christ are *with Christ.*

Far more important than understanding the nature of the afterlife is having an assurance of its reality. The New Testament is very sketchy about the state of life after death, but is full and emphatic about the importance of Christian hope of eternal life. Paul's words do not tell us much about the condition of the dead in Christ, but his words tell us much about the strength and influence of his hope.

In this respect Paul is worlds apart from those who claim that whether or not a person believes in life after death is irrelevant. They are agnostics not only about the nature of an afterlife but about the reality of any kind of afterlife. Then they say: "Besides, what difference does it make? A person can live a good, decent, and useful life whether or not he believes in life after death." Often they go a step further to justify their own position: "Belief in life after death makes people fail to give their best to this life. Their hope makes them so otherworldly that they neither can enjoy what life offers nor do their part to make this a better place to live."

There is a kind of otherworldliness of which these charges are true, but the charges are not true of the biblical hope. Christian hope is not irrelevant. Paul was ready to die, but he also was ready to live. In fact, he was ready to live precisely because he served Christ who made him equally ready for life or for death. Verses 24-26 show that Paul's confident hope had not diminished his zest for life. He was ready to go to be with the Lord; he was equally ready to stay and serve God by helping the Philippians. For him life meant "fruitful labor" (1:22). It meant serving God and others. This gave life meaning, purpose, and joy.

All of this was rooted in Paul's view of life and death. His life was rooted in Christ. He had been caught up in the eternal purpose of God. What he did contributed to that eternal purpose. Circumstances could not defeat that purpose; even the final enemy of humanity, death itself, could not thwart that purpose. This outlook freed Paul from all the selfish and petty pursuits that sap human energy and divert attention from what life is all about. This hope freed Paul from the shackles of that multitude of anxieties and fears which rob humans of the courage to live as they were intended to.

Like the song says, many people are "tired of living but scared of dying." F. B. Meyer in his devotional commentary on Philippians contrasts Paul's words in this passage with Hamlet's words in his famous soliloquy.[6] Hamlet like Paul weighed life and death. Life had become so unbearable that he seriously contemplated suicide. Yet the uncertainties and terrors of death made this option even more undesirable than continuing to face the unbearable realities of life.

There are some similarities between Paul and Hamlet. Both weighed life and death, and both turned from death to life. But there the similarities end. Hamlet weighed life and death and found both undesirable, life only slightly less so. Paul weighed the issues of life and death and found them both desirable. He had no fear of death because dying was to depart and be with Christ. On the other hand, he had continuing zest for living, for life provided continued opportunities of serving God and helping others.

Bill Wallace was just an ordinary man, but he lived an extraordinary life because he shared this Christian philosophy of life. He went to the Orient as a medical missionary and labored for fifteen years in that sea of human need called China. As a skilled surgeon, he brought help and healing to sick and broken bodies. As a representative of the Great Physician, he shared the gospel of salvation. Then under communist oppression he was called upon to give all a man can give—his life. The communist government discouraged any display of remembrance, but the Chinese people who knew Bill Wallace best erected over his grave a marker pointing heavenward. Because they had seen Christ in his living and in his dying, they placed this appropriate inscription on the marker: "For to me to live is Christ."[7]

3

Christian Togetherness

Philippians 1:27 to 2:4

Most parents whose children are away from home in college have received letters that are more than just information. Such letters often begin with personal greetings and a hopeful inquiry about the well-being of everyone at home. Then there is usually an account of the recent activities at college. The real purpose for the letter, however, comes to light when the reader reaches such words as these: "By the way I'm running a little short this month. Could you send me an extra check?"

In most personal letters the writer has some purpose in mind. It may be merely to send greetings or to supply information, but often the purpose runs deeper. This was the case with Paul's letter to Philippi; his purpose is revealed in Philippians 1:27 to 2:4.

As we saw in chapter 1, students of Philippians have suggested several possible reasons for the letter. Some have seen it as a letter designed to express the apostle's gratitude for the help he had received. Although there is no doubt that he used the letter as an occasion for expressing his thanks, there are problems in accepting this theory as the best explanation of Paul's main purpose.

There is, for instance, the question, "Why did Paul wait so long to thank them?" Considerable time had elapsed since Epaphroditus had come to Rome, and it would not have been like Paul to have waited so long to express his appreciation. It is, in fact, even possible that he wrote a letter of thanks to them immediately after Epaphroditus arrived. At any rate, he wrote with deeper intent than to express long-overdue gratitude.

Another suggestion is that Paul's purpose was purely informative: all sorts of rumors and reports had reached Philippi, so Paul wrote to supply the believers with an accurate description of the conditions of his imprisonment. It cannot be denied that Paul did use the letter to inform the Philippians concerning himself and Epaphroditus. Few students of Philippians, however, believe that this desire to supply information was Paul's main reason for writing.

The letter contains unmistakable evidences of Paul's concern for the fellowship of the church. The note of recurring joy in the letter is somewhat dimmed by an apparent undercurrent of trouble in Philippi. For example, there had been some sort of falling out between two prominent women in the church (4:2). In addressing the beloved Philippians, Paul even found it necessary to warn of the dangers of murmurings and disputings (2:14).

The passage before us is the heart of the Philippian letter. Personal greetings are behind him, and Paul has told of his circumstances. Now he comes to say what is on his heart. He had apparently heard of this undercurrent in the church. It had not yet reached serious enough proportions to cause the apostle to deal with it so sternly as he had had to do in the case of Corinth. There was enough danger, however, to inspire Paul to make this plea for Christian togetherness.

We can be thankful that he did, for these words are a ringing challenge to modern churches. There is a sense in which disruptive dissension is a danger to any healthy church. Just as a person must take certain steps to guard his physical health, so must the body of Christ take every precaution to guard its spiritual health. It is also important to remember that Christian togetherness is not just the absence of wrangling among the members; true Christian fellowship is a positive relationship in which there is room for continuous growth. All of us, therefore, need to give serious heed to Paul's plea for Christian togetherness.

Side by Side (1:27-30)

Paul had already had one tragic experience with faction in a church, and he did not relish the thought of another. The spirit of pride that had torn the fellowship in Corinth left its scars on many lives—including Paul's. The whole mess had left the apostle so distraught that he even passed up opportunities to preach when the crisis was at its peak (2 Cor. 2:12-13). Anyone who has been involved in a similar crisis knows that nothing so undercuts the gospel as a proud, factious spirit among professing Christians.

Paul saw in Philippi a potential Corinth; he saw among his beloved Philippians the first budding of the same pride that had burst into full bloom in Corinth. How it must have frightened him to remember the way believers in Corinth had divided into warring camps over the supposed loyalty to one of several leaders (1 Cor. 1:12-13). With a shudder he must have recalled the mockery the Corinthians had made of their so-called worship services (1 Cor. 11:18).

The Corinthians, however, had nothing on some churches today. There are those who think little or nothing of splitting a church fellowship. A church is supposed to be mounting a mighty offensive against the entrenched forces of evil; instead a band of believers chooses up sides and fights a civil war. Usually some issue arises over which there is disagreement. Often the issue at stake is something trivial, but someone gets his feelings hurt. Soon people begin to take sides, and the fight is on. The struggle often focuses on the business meetings of the church, but one can sense the hard feelings in every aspect of church life.

The ultimate results of a church feud are disastrous. A church is supposed to be a spiritual home to nurture believers. Instead it becomes a hotbed of bad feelings that chill their faith and stunt their spiritual growth.

Then think what an effect all of this has on those outside the church. Those who have always claimed that the church is filled with hypocrites are supplied with evidence to back up their argument. Others who are more sincere have an almost unavoidable stumbling block thrown across their paths. Could there be any more false witness to real Christianity than pride and faction? No wonder one of Paul's sharpest indictments is laid against those who would disrupt the fellowship of a church (1 Cor. 3:17).

With this in mind we can better understand why Paul said what he did in Philippians 1:27. The translation in the King James Version obscures the real meaning of Paul's words. The word "conversation" meant more in 1611 than it does today; for the word it translates describes one's whole way of life, not just his words. The word means literally "conduct as a citizen." The noun form of the root is found in Philippians 3:20, where Paul reminded them that their citizenship is in heaven. In 1:27 he was appealing to them to conduct themselves as citizens of the heavenly kingdom.

This would have had special meaning to the Philippians because they took pride in the fact that their city was a colony of Rome. This was a real honor for a city in the first century. Many of the early settlers of Philippi had been Roman army veterans, who had passed on their proud tradition to their descendants. The inhabitants were citizens of Rome; the city was laid out on the pattern of a miniature Rome; and the customs and institutions were Roman. The people, therefore, proudly tried to pattern themselves after the Roman model. Paul reminded the believers in Philippi that they were, first of all, citizens of heaven and should model their lives accordingly.

When the early European settlers came to the new world, they set up colonies that reflected their homelands across the sea. Whether they were English, French, or Spanish was apparent to a visitor who was familiar with the homeland. For example, the British colonies along the Atlantic coast of North America reflected the language, customs, and institutions of Great Britain. Here was a bit of the British Isles transplanted on new soil.

In the same way, a church is a colony of heaven, and its members should easily be recognized as citizens of the heavenly kingdom. Their attitudes and actions should make this plain; their words and deeds should bear witness to the King who rules their lives.

Paul's use of this word is significant for another reason. There was another word for conduct meaning "to walk" that he used more frequently (Eph. 4:1). Paul apparently used the word with the idea of citizenship to remind the Philippians of "their *mutual* duties as members of a local Christian commonwealth."[1] Because the word had a social context, the apostle could use it to remind them that worthy Christian conduct involved one's relations with his brothers in Christ. The New Testament teaches that a person cannot really love God without loving his brothers in Christ.

Two books with similar settings are *Robinson Crusoe* and *Swiss Family Robinson.* Both tell of the efforts of survivors of shipwrecks at sea to maintain their lives on lonely islands. The obvious difference, however, is that Robinson Crusoe was alone while the others were a family. There is an analogy here to a church. The Christian is no Robinson Crusoe struggling alone against fear and loneliness; he is more like a member of Swiss Family Robinson dependent on the family relation to survive in a hostile environment.

Paul's purpose to appeal for Christian togetherness is evident in his admonition to "stand firm in one spirit, with one mind striving side by side for the faith of the gospel" (1:27). Notice the emphasis on the words "one" and "side by side." The apostle's words show that he was convinced that a church which stands in *one* spirit and strives *side by side* can do all things for Christ's sake.

He did not minimize the terror of the adversaries that confronted them or the conflicts through which they must pass. There are foes to face and trials to bear, but a strongly united Christian fellowship can defeat any evil and endure any trial.

Paul's words suggest two analogies—Christians are like soldiers and athletes. The word translated "stand firm" suggests soldiers standing resolutely together against an enemy. The word translated "striving side by side" was often used to describe striving in a contest or game in the arena. In fact, we get our word "athlete" from the root of the latter word. Paul used the simple verb form of *athleo* in 2 Timothy 2:5, where he described contending in the games for the victor's crown. In classical Greek this word was used also of contending in battle. Since many athletic contests involved gladiators fighting for their lives, the striving of soldiers in battle and athletes in the arena were not so different.

The word in Philippians 1:27 is a form of *sunathleo*, created by adding the prefix meaning "together with" to *athleo*. Paul was thinking not of an individual standing and striving alone either on the battlefield or in the arena; he was picturing a contest in which success depends on standing together and striving side by side for the gospel.

One commentator notes of Philippians 1:27: "Here the metaphor seems to be drawn . . . from the combats of the Roman amphitheatre. Like criminals or captives, the believers are condemned to fight for their lives: against them are arrayed the ranks of worldliness and sin: only unflinching courage and steady combination can win the victory against such odds."[2]

It is probably significant that the only two New Testament uses of this word are in Philippians (1:27; 4:3). In both instances Paul was writing about Christians standing and striving side by side. In Philippians 4:3 the context shows that Paul was calling on his readers to turn from disruptive dissension and to recapture the spirit of togetherness inherent in their commitment to Christ. This also is the strong implication of Paul's words in 1:27.

Also in the background of Philippians 1:27-30 is some form of opposition and persecution. Paul's point in verse 28 is that his readers need not fear any form of outward opposition if they stand together with oneness of mind and spirit. Their opponents cannot defeat them when they do this. The New Testament consistently maintains that even when hostile forces do their worst, they cannot destroy Christian faith and love. Opponents can imprison, torture, and even kill Christians; but they cannot defeat Christian faith.

Luke 21:18 is a striking statement of this truth. Jesus had just described how persecutors would kill his followers. Then he said, "But not a hair on your head will perish." In this graphic way Jesus assured his disciples that even death could not ultimately defeat them or his cause. This is also Paul's point in the inspiring and assuring words of Romans 8:35-39. Nothing can defeat the power of Christian love. Thus the opponents in Philippians 1:28 would see two clear portents in the unity of Christians as they faced persecution: "This is a clear omen to them of their destruction, but of your salvation, and that from God."

We do not know what kind or degree of persecution was going on in Philippi. Little is said about persecution elsewhere in the letter. Apparently they were not going through the kind of severe persecution reflected in some New Testament writings (for example, Acts 4—5; 7—9; 12; 1 Pet. 3—4; Rev. 2—3). Probably the situation in Philippi was that faced by all Christians in the early centuries—being a misunderstood minority in a potentially hostile society. Paul had been beaten and imprisoned on his first visit to Philippi. The same forces of unbelief, prejudice, and greed were still in control of Philippian society. As a result, believers always were subject to opposition of some kind.

Verse 29 shows that Paul regarded suffering for Christ as a privilege, not a burden: "For it has been granted to you that for the sake of Christ you should not only believe in him but also suffer for his sake." The word translated "granted" is the verb form of the Greek word for "grace." That is, God's free and gracious gift includes the privilege not only of believing in Christ but also of suffering for him.

This is consistent with what the Bible elsewhere teaches about suffering. There is no attempt to explain it. Rather there is simply the affirmation that suffering for Christ's sake lies within the will of a gracious God whom we can trust.

Some commentators believe there were those in the Philippian church who would not accept suffering as a Christian's lot. Ralph Martin suggests that their reaction to unexpected suffering was a factor in the complaining and disputing in the church (2:14): "The chief thrust of Paul's answer is to show that God's plan includes the suffering of the churches (1:29) and how the nature of the Christian calling gets its model from the incarnate Lord himself (2:6-11). He came to his exaltation along a road of self-humbling, rejection, and obedience unto death."[3]

Paul also referred the Philippians to his own experience as a sufferer for Christ's sake. Paul told the Philippians that when they were suffering for Christ's sake, they were "engaged in the same conflict which you saw and now hear to be mine" (1:30). They had witnessed the persecution that befell Paul in Philippi, and they had heard of his current imprisonment. Whatever they suffered for Christ's sake was part of the same larger conflict or struggle in which they and Paul shared.

The word translated "conflict" in verse 30 is a word applied originally to a contest in the arena. It came to be used in a broader sense of any struggle. The same word is used in 1 Timothy 6:12 ("Fight the good fight of faith.") and 2 Timothy 4:7 ("I have fought the good fight."). *The Good News Bible* preserves the athletic analogy in 2 Timothy 4:7: "I have done my best in the race." However, in Philippians 1:30 the translation sounds more military: "Now you can take part with me in the battle. It is the same battle you saw me fighting in the past, and as you hear, the one I am fighting still."[4]

There is a sense in which a church is like an athletic team. The individual Christian's life may be compared to a form of athletic contest in which it is every man for himself, but a more appropriate analogy is that of a group of athletes in team competition. The nature of the Christian life is such that a person must be on a team to compete in the game of life.

A church needs a team spirit in which all the members work together for the good of the team, and no one strives to be a "glory hog." A winning team is one that works together. There may be outstanding athletes on the team, but they function as a part of the team.

A star passer would be helpless without a good line to block and useless without capable backs and ends to receive the passes. A good pitcher would be helpless without fielders. When Lefty Gomez was asked the secret of his success as a pitcher, he replied, "Clean living and a fast outfield."

Nothing can spell such sure disaster for a team as a lack of team spirit; on the other hand, a group with *esprit de corps* can often defeat a more talented team lacking a spirit of cooperation. What is the "warmth" that characterizes some churches? It is the sense of belonging together that results in caring for one another and working together for the cause of Christ.

As we have seen, the words translated "striving side by side" (1:27) and "conflict" (1:30) also had a military connotation. There are many passages in the Bible in which the Christian life is pictured as a spiritual warfare (cf. Eph. 6:12). Whatever the analogy Paul intended in Philippians 1:27-30, the point is that believers must stand together against the aggressive forces of evil. There is continuing truth in the saying, "United we stand; divided we fall." If Christians are to overcome evil, we need the strength God gives us through brothers and sisters in Christ.

Never has the United States of America faced such peril as when we were at war with ourselves. It was during those dark days of the Civil War when brother often fought brother that the American dream was most threatened with disaster. Likewise, never is a church so imperiled as when there is civil war within the fellowship.

Visitors to the National Park on the site of the Battle of Shiloh find it hard to believe that thousands of men fought and died in those quiet woods and fields. Historians remind us that there is good reason for the name "bloody Shiloh," which survivors on both sides applied to the battle. In the exhibit room at Park Headquarters are the words with which the commanding Federal general, Ulysses S. Grant, appraised the battle. Grant wrote, "The troops on both sides were American, and united they need not fear any foreign foe."[5]

If Americans can really learn the lesson that Grant drew from the battle, perhaps those brave men will not have died in vain. If Christians can learn the same lesson in the church fellowship, then Paul will not have written in vain. Is this not what Paul was saying of a church—united we need not fear any foe?

Oneness Without Sameness (2:1-4)

Because he believed this, Paul appealed to every worthy motive in his plea for Christian togetherness: "So if there is any encouragement in Christ, any incentive of love, any participation in the Spirit, any affection and sympathy, complete my joy by being of the same mind, having the same love, being in full accord and of one mind" (2:1-2).

The word "so" ties these verses inseparably to the preceding verses. Actually Paul picks up and elaborates on his plea in 1:27. Some commentators say that 1:27-30 focuses on external opposition while 2:1-4 deals with internal dissension. This misses the main theme that runs throughout—Paul's plea for Christian togetherness. The persecution theme in 1:28-30 is secondary, not primary. Marvin Vincent paraphrases the main theme like this: " 'I have exhorted you to stand fast in one spirit; to strive with one mind for the faith of the gospel, unterrified by your adversaries. *Therefore*, complete my joy by being of one accord and avoiding faction and vainglory.' "6

Verse 1 shows that the heart of Christian faith and experience moves believers in the direction of Christian togetherness. Paul based his appeal on four aspects of Christian experience. The first and third of these refer to what we have and are in Christ and in his Spirit. The second and fourth emphasize what we receive in and through Christ—love, affection, and sympathy.

Paul appealed, first of all, to the life in Christ as an encouragement. The phrase "in Christ" means more than the presence of the living Christ in the heart of each individual believer (see comments on 1:1). It refers also to the union with Christ which all believers share. Christ is in each believer, and all believers are in Christ. This is similar to the term Paul used to describe the church—the body of Christ.

A similar idea of sharing the divine life is contained in Paul's appeal based on being participants in the same Spirit. The word translated "participation" is *koinonia*, which stresses our sharing of one life in our common relationship with Christ through his Spirit.

Paul's point is that togetherness is inherent in Christian experience. We believe in, pray to, and seek to do the will of one heavenly Father. How can we do so except as brothers? The sons of the same Father are brothers and should act as such.

We trust and serve the same Lord and Savior. This means we all have come as sinners to the level ground at the foot of the cross. And we have acknowledged the same Lord and Master. Everything about this draws together. We cannot come to Christ without coming at the same time to others who come to Christ.

We have experienced the same Spirit. The New Testament uses different terminology—Spirit, Holy Spirit, Spirit of God, Spirit of Christ—to express the same reality. The gifts of the Spirit differ, but the Spirit is the same.

Paul made the same point in considerably more detail in 1 Corinthians 12. There he acknowledged the diversity of those who are baptized by one Spirit into one body—the body of Christ. First Corinthians 12, therefore, is an excellent commentary on Paul's words to the Philippians. This is not surprising if the problems in Corinth and Philippi were similar. The obvious problem was disruptive dissension brought on by selfishness and pride. Philippians 2:1-4 shows that this also was a problem in Philippi, although not yet so far advanced as it had become in Corinth. In both instances Paul stressed our common life in Christ through his Spirit.

Also in both instances Paul stressed Christian love, *agape*. Philippians 1:1 reflects the same idea found not only in 1 Corinthians 12 but also in 1 Corinthians 13, the famous love chapter. In Philippians 2:1 Paul appealed to the "incentive of love" and to "affection and sympathy." No theme in the New Testament is so clear as this: Christ has loved us and given himself for us; therefore we are to love and give ourselves for one another.

No serious reader of these verses from Philippians can deny that Paul is calling for some sort of Christian togetherness; but the question is, What is the meaning of "being of the same mind, having the same love, being in full accord and of one mind" (2:2)? What is the nature of the Christian togetherness for which Paul was pleading?

First of all, be careful to distinguish Christian togetherness from that kind of conformity which reduces an individual to nothing more than a regimented member of a group. Paul's repetition of the words "one" and "same" does not refer to sameness. There can be oneness without sameness. This was Paul's point in 1 Corinthians 12: the body of Christ has a oneness of common life that is expressed in a diversity of ways.

Marriage is an appropriate analogy. The biblical view of marriage assumes a basic oneness of shared life together, but it does not mean the loss of individuality. Paradoxically, the richest marriages are those that provide a couple maximum commitment to one another and maximum freedom to be themselves. As someone has said: "In a marriage in which two people always agree, one of the two is unnecessary."

Paul's analogy of the body makes the same point. The oneness of the body depends on the healthy functioning of the diverse parts. As applied to the church, Paul wanted each member to do two things: (1) Discover and express his own distinctive gifts. (2) Encourage others to discover and express their own distinctive gifts. All the members are important; all are interdependent.

Let us beware the cult of conformity that would rob persons of their individuality. This is not the kind of Christian togetherness sought in a church; in fact, it is opposed to the principles of Christ. Regimentation tends to reduce people to impersonal parts of an organization, to numbers and statistics.

Real togetherness must be distinguished not only from regimentation and conformity but also from "fellowship" and "cooperation." Togetherness includes fellowship and cooperation, but it is a much richer concept than what we ordinarily mean by these words. As we have seen, the word translated "participation" in verse 1 is better transliterated than translated; there is no English word that adequately translates *koinonia*. We speak of "fellowship," but this word has too often been identified with socials and suppers. This can be a valid and important expression of *koinonia*, but it is too narrow a definition to do it justice. "Fellowship" may at times be the best English word to translate *koinonia*, but let us be careful not to limit *koinonia* to what some people mean by fellowship.

Another popular word is "cooperation." This has come to be one of the most hallowed words in Christian circles, and no doubt it should be. However, we should not equate *koinonia* with cooperation. Even a group of criminals can cooperate in an evil scheme if they stand to gain thereby. Christian cooperation grows out of richer soil than a common purpose. *Koinonia* describes essentially a shared life in Christ. The best analogy is that of a family. We are brothers and sisters in Christ because we share a common faith in God our Father.

Several years ago a social scientist named David Riessman wrote a book entitled *The Lonely Crowd.* This is an appropriate title to describe a time in which people live closer together than ever before but are also more lonely than ever. Even in the big cities and in the big organizations, people feel alone.

Is there no help for such loneliness? A real spirit of Christian togetherness is the answer. A Christian church is the answer to the lonely crowd. We must beware letting our churches become just the opposite—large organizations in which persons become only numbers and statistics. No church, large or small, can spend too much energy seeking a warmer spirit of Christian togetherness.

Paul knew that such a spirit must be cultivated; therefore he admonished the Philippians to shun pride at all costs. Like a medical research scientist who has isolated the cause of some dread disease, Paul holds up the villain for all to see. Pride is the villain, the kind of pride that causes faction and strife. Paul had seen what it did in Corinth, and he wanted to spare the beloved brothers in Philippi such a trial. He therefore, pled, "Do nothing from selfishness or conceit" (2:3).

Scholars debate the exact meaning of the word translated "selfishness." It was used at times by the Greeks to refer to that kind of selfish ambition that stoops to any means to get what it wants. On the other hand, it may be kin to a word meaning strife, discord, contention, dissension. Thus the word may refer either to selfish ambition or to the strife that inevitably results from the collision of interests of persons driven by selfish ambition.

The word translated "conceit" combines two words meaning "empty" and "glory," thus the King James Version "vainglory." The word refers to the strutting, empty pretentiousness of excessive and selfish pride.

Pride more than anything else destroys *koinonia*. Pride is the belief that I am better than I am and the attempt to act in the light of that vain delusion. According to the Bible, selfish conceit is the basic human sin that afflicts humanity. This was the sin of Adam and Eve, and it is our sin. It separates us from God, disrupts our relations with others, and robs us of life as it was meant to be lived.

Selfish conceit is so deeply entrenched in human life and society that it continues to be the basic sin of people even after they experience God's saving grace. Nothing is so contradictory to Christ and his way; yet we must continue to struggle with this subtle and deadly sin all our lives. Only God's continuing grace and power can save us from this plight.

No one can deny that "me-sickness" is deeply rooted in modern life. There has been a valid emphasis on self-fulfillment. Given a proper context of faith in God and love toward others, self-fulfillment is healthy and positive. God wants each of us to find abundant life. However, many people interpret self-fulfillment as their one guideline for living. That is, *my* wants and needs take precedence over everything else—God, church, society, even family. Nothing and no one has any right to ask me to give up anything that is important in my quest for happiness and fulfillment. *My* needs. *My* wants. *My* attainments. These are what count. The King James translation "vainglory" is appropriate for such blind folly and littleness of spirit.

Over against this Paul set "humility" or "lowliness of mind." He wrote, "In humility count others better than yourselves" (2:3). In Greek usage the word "humility," and others like it, generally were used in a disparaging way. "Lowliness" for them meant subjection to something or someone else, and by their standards this was not a desirable quality. By biblical and Christian standards, however, lowliness of mind is a quality to be sought. The Old Testament prescribes submission as the proper attitude of creature before Creator. Jesus taught humble service as the proper attitude toward God and others. He challenged the world's standard of greatness when measured by such things as wealth, power, and prestige. He substituted a paradoxical standard of greatness based on humble service to others: " 'He who is greatest among you shall be your servant; whoever exalts himself will be humbled, and whoever humbles himself will be exalted' " (Matt. 23:11-12).

Genuine faith in God and love to others is inevitably expressed also in humility with regard to oneself. This is the exact opposite of the selfish conceit that assumes the world must revolve around *me*. I am a creature of God in a world of other creatures. I am a child of God in a family of brothers. Therefore, I am not unimportant, but my importance is in the context of my relationship to God and others. I am not God; neither am I alone in God's world or family. And it is sheer folly to act as if I were.

What did Paul mean when he wrote, "Count others better than yourselves"? Is this a proof-text for someone with an inferiority complex? There are people who feel worthless and useless, but persons of faith should not feel this way. God's love in Christ shows that each person is of great value. God's gift of the Spirit imparts spiritual gifts to all his people. Thus Paul was not talking about an inferiority complex or that kind of bogus humility that depreciates one's worth or usefulness to God and others.

Verse 4 continues the thought from the last part of verse 3: "Let each of you look not only to his own interests, but also to the interests of others." Romans 12:3 makes a similar point in slightly different words: "I bid every one among you not to think of himself more highly than he ought to think." Paul followed up on this verse in Romans with the analogy of the church as one body with many members. This analogy is developed more fully in 1 Corinthians 12. We have already noted the probable similarity in background between the letter to the Philippians and 1 Corinthians. Some in the Corinthian church were acting as if they were superior or more important than others. Paul did not deny their value and importance. Each person and his spiritual gift is important; just as each member of the human body is important. But it is folly for one member to assume that he is the whole body or that he can get along without the others. The application to the togetherness of a church congregation is obvious.

What Paul is calling for here is the recognition of the talents and gifts of others in God's kingdom. We attain to mature faith and humility when we recognize and perform our own part in the church while recognizing the parts played by our brothers in Christ. Our own part does not, thereby, become unimportant; but it is seen in its proper relation to others in the cause of the Lord.

Back in the days of pump organs a famous musician presented a concert in a certain city. While he played the keyboard before the assembled throng, a boy pumped the organ behind the instrument. At the intermission when the organist took his bow, he was surprised to hear a ripple of laughter. Glancing back, he saw that the boy had stepped out onto the stage and was taking a bow also. The proud musician shoved him out of sight saying, "I'm the one they are applauding." When he returned shortly to the organ for the second half of the concert, the musician was surprised to find that the organ made no sound. Looking frantically behind the organ, he found the boy sitting with his arms folded. With a defiant look the youth said, "Next time say '*We* are the ones they are applauding.' " All of us need the reminder the organist received that night.

This is what Paul is saying: A Christian is to do his best, but he is to give the credit to God and others for what good is accomplished. In a tight football game a tackle was to throw the key block. He did his job and looked up from the muddy field to see the quarterback cross the goal line almost untouched. The eyes of everyone were on the man who made the score. Few people noticed the tackle at the bottom of the pile of heavy, helmeted men. The big fellow, however, got to his feet and was the first to join in hoisting the star runner to his shoulders amidst the cheers of the crowd. This is Christian humility.

George Whitefield and John Wesley were responsible more than any two men for the great Evangelical Revival of the eighteenth century. Doctrinal disagreements, however, tended to separate the two men in later years. Whitefield was much more of a Calvinist than was Wesley. The two men, in spite of this, continued to hold one another in high regard. Some of their disciples who lacked the deep commitment of either man tried to increase the personal differences between the two leaders. One such man once asked George Whitefield if he thought he would see John Wesley in heaven. "No, Sir!" replied the great preacher, "He will be so near the throne and we at such distance that we shall hardly get a sight of him."[7] That is true humility.

4

Christ—the Way

Philippians 2:5-11

Tom Skinner wrote a book with this intriguing title, *If Christ Is the Answer, What Are the Questions?*[1] We Christians believe that Jesus Christ is the answer to the most basic human questions: How can I know God? What can I do with my guilt? Where can I find meaning, strength, and direction for living? How can I relate to others as I should? What about death and dying?

The New Testament presents Christ as the Way—not only the Way to eternal life but also the Way to abundant living. The proclamation of the exalted Christ is linked with the directions and help Christ provides for daily living.

Philippians 2:5-11 is an excellent example of Paul's view of Christ as the Way. On the one hand, no passage presents a more exalted description of Jesus Christ; on the other hand, this description is part of Paul's practical challenge to the Philippian church. Philippians 2:5-11 is a crucial part of the same theme begun in 1:27 and spelled out so clearly in 2:1-4. As was noted in the last chapter, Paul warned against the spirit of disruptive dissension that is the inevitable result of selfish pride. He called for a spirit of Christian togetherness based on Christian humility and love. Paul's point in 2:5-11 is that the humble way of self-giving love is at the heart of the Christian proclamation. Not only did Jesus teach this as the way to live, but he also powerfully depicted this way in all that he was and did.

Sharing the Mind of Christ (2:5)

In the early morning hours of April 15, 1865 a great man lay dying in a little room in a house on Tenth Street in Washington, D.C.

President Abraham Lincoln had been shot the preceding night while he watched a performance at Ford's Theater. He had been carried across the street to the room in which he lay all that night. When the President died at 7:20 AM, Secretary of War Edwin Stanton pulled down the window shade to shut out the bright morning sun and said, "Now he belongs to the ages."

There is another of whom these words are true in a more absolute sense than they are of Abraham Lincoln. There is one of whom it may be said not only that he belongs to the ages but also that the ages belong to him. The influence of a great man like Lincoln does outlive his brief earthly sojourn, but there is a greater one whose influence shapes all of history. Indeed, Jesus Christ is the center and key to the eternal plan of God.

Verses 6-11 present a poetic description of the contrast between the humble circumstances of Jesus' earthly sojourn and the exalted state of the heavenly Lord. Few passages in the New Testament have received such careful study. Lengthy theological debates have centered on the meaning of single words. In dealing with this passage scholars continue to probe, wonder, and not always to agree.

Two points of scholarly debate are these: (1) Was this passage originally composed as a hymn? (2) Was the purpose primarily to challenge the Philippians to imitate Christ or to proclaim Christ as the cosmic Lord?

Many scholars believe that verses 6-11 were part of a hymn. Paul could have been quoting a Christian hymn written by someone else or one he himself had written earlier. Or he could have composed a hymn or poem as part of this letter. Paul apparently felt that the lyrical quality of poetic language was suited for the exalted subject of which he wrote.

The real debate over this passage centers not so much around whether or not this was a hymn or poem; the real question is "What point does the hymn make?" The traditional view has been that these verses present Christ's example of humble love as a challenge to the Philippians. Another view is that the hymn focuses on the lordship of Christ as a challenge to the Philippians. Ralph P. Martin, for example, summarizes the message in this way: "Let your relationships in the Christian community be such as show that they are conducted in the sphere of this new humanity of which Christ Jesus is Lord and in which we are members who, in allegiance and confession, proclaim that lordship."[2]

Perhaps we are not forced to exclude completely either of these views. The traditional view draws heavily on verses 6-8, and the other view looks mostly to verses 9-11. Whatever may have been predominant in Paul's mind, both ideas are true. Both also fit the context, although the traditional view seems to fit more closely with verses 1-4.

In any case, verse 5 is the obvious connection between verses 1-4 and 6-11. Unfortunately, the exact meaning of this verse is debated. There is no verb in the last part of the verse. Translators ordinarily supply a verb, depending on how they interpret the words "in Christ Jesus." The King James Version assumes that "in Christ Jesus" refers to "in the experience of Jesus Christ"(v. 5): "Let this mind be in you, which was also in Christ Jesus." *Today's English Version* follows this same assumption: "The attitude you should have is the one Christ Jesus had" (TEV).

By contrast, the Revised Standard Version assumes that "in Christ Jesus" refers to the experience of believers who are "in Christ Jesus": "Have this mind among yourselves, which you have in Christ Jesus." *The New English Bible* is based on the same assumption: "Let your bearing towards one another arise out of your life in Christ Jesus."

The latter view is based on Paul's normal use of the words "in Christ." He began the Philippian letter by referring to his readers as "saints in Christ Jesus" (1:1). The phrase refers not only to the individual's personal union with the Spirit of Christ but also to the consequent relationship of those who know Christ. Paul had just appealed for Christian togetherness based on several similar motivations, including "encouragement in Christ" (2:1). In verse 5 he picked up this key point and set the stage for elaborating on it in verses 6-11.

This interpretation does not rule out the idea of following Christ's example. However, it goes beyond what we ordinarily mean by following a high and noble example. On the one hand, it is unquestionably true that Jesus Christ is the perfect model or example of how life is to be lived (see 1 Peter 2:21). On the other hand, being a Christian means much more than trying to follow Christ's example.

Paul's point was not that Jesus Christ was merely our example and inspiration. He is that, but he is far more: a commitment to Christ brings the believer into contact with a life-changing presence. Paul was not exhorting the Philippians merely to follow the example of Christ; he was calling on them to share the mind of Christ made possible by being in Christ. Paul left as his own testimony these words from the Galatian letter: "I have been crucified with Christ; it is no longer I who live, but Christ who lives in me; and the life I now live in the flesh I live by faith in the Son of God, who loved me and gave himself for me" (Gal. 2:20).

Joseph Parker was a pastor in New England during the days when the Unitarian movement was most aggressive. Many people were saying that Jesus was only a great man who set a good example for mankind to follow. Parker often asked them what good it would do for Christ merely to set before us an ideal that we could not attain. He used the example of Paderewski and his piano. Would it be possible to play like Paderewski just by hearing him play? It would not matter how much one was inspired by the example of the great master; he could not be inspired enough to share his ability. The only possibility of playing like Paderewski, so Parker would say, would be if the great musician could somehow become incarnate in a person and, thereby, share his ability with the person in whom he dwelt. This, of course, is preposterously impossible in the case of Paderewski; but there is one who can become incarnate in human life. That one is the living Lord whose Spirit comes into open hearts to enable us to live as Jesus did in the days of his flesh.

Living under the lordship of Christ means taking seriously the teachings of Jesus and the example of Jesus as he lived those teachings. But this presupposes a personal commitment to and a personal experience with Jesus Christ. God's grace in Christ frees a person from the chains of guilt and failure. His Spirit inspires and enables believers to live a new life. Jesus Christ makes possible the pardon, pattern, and power for that new life. He is the model for that life, and his abiding presence is the power for that life. He who overcame temptation is with us to help us overcome. He who put God's will first is with us to help us do the same. He who gave himself in humble service for others is with us to help us act with self-giving humility and love.

Jesus Christ is not only with *each* of us on a personal and individual level; he is with *all* of us who know him. Thus he works in and through the corporate experience of Christians as Christ's body. He instructs, inspires, and encourages us through one another. He works in each of us and in all of us to help us follow that pattern of life of which he is the only perfect example. This is what Paul meant by sharing the mind of Christ.

The Humble Self-Giving of Christ (2:6-8)

Scholars do not agree on how the hymn in verses 6-11 is laid out at every point, but they do agree on its two main parts. Verses 6-8 present the humble self-giving of Christ; verses 9-11 describe the exaltation of Jesus Christ.

Paul referred to Christ Jesus as the one "who, though he was in the form of God, did not count equality with God a thing to be grasped, but emptied himself, taking the form of a servant, being born in the likeness of men" (2:6-7). Most interpreters see this as a reference to Christ laying aside his preexistent glory in order to assume the humble status of a human being. Marvin R. Vincent paraphrases the meaning this way: "For, he, though he existed from eternity in a state of equality with God, did not regard that divine condition of being as one might regard a prize to be eagerly grasped, but laid it aside, and took the form of a bondservant, having been made in the likeness of men."[3]

The words of Paul reflect the preexistent glory of Christ. When the apostle wrote of Christ existing in the "form" of God, he used a word meaning "essential likeness." Paul also noted that Christ had an equality with God the Father.

This teaching is even more explicit in other passages of the New Testament, particularly in the Gospel of John. The Fourth Gospel begins with a verse reminiscent of Genesis 1:1. The Gospel writer maintained that Jesus Christ is the eternal Word who shares the very nature of God. Later in the same Gospel there is a debate between Jesus and his opponents in which the Savior makes the same claim. Jesus had told them that any man who kept his word would never taste death. This had provoked his enemies to ask him if he were claiming to be greater than the men of God of the past like Abraham, all of whom were dead. Jesus replied, " 'Your father Abraham rejoiced that he was to see my day; he saw it and was glad' " (John 8:56). With rising impatience they demanded to know how he who was not yet fifty years old could claim to have seen Abraham. Jesus made this brief reply: " 'Before Abraham was, I am' " (John 8:58). In his prayer for believers recorded in the seventeenth chapter of John, Jesus referred to this glory which he shared with the Father before the foundation of the world (John 17:5).

John is not the only one to testify to Christ's incarnate glory. Hebrews 1:2 refers to Christ as God's Son whom God "appointed the heir of all things, through whom also he created the world." In Colossians 1:15-16 Paul used similar language in describing the preexistent Christ.

Paul's words bid us note how Christ did not conceive of this exalted status as something to be selfishly grasped for himself; but rather he emptied himself, took the form of a slave, and became a man. The apostle elsewhere summed up this idea in these words: "For you know the grace of our Lord Jesus Christ, that though he was rich, yet for your sake he became poor, so that by his poverty you might become rich" (2 Cor. 8:9). The Son of God, who shared the eternal glory of the Father, laid aside his heavenly glory and became a man.

Paul's description of the humility displayed in this descent calls to mind the familiar stories of the Savior's birth, recorded in Matthew and Luke. There we see the actual story of what happened when the eternal Son of God became flesh. There are tokens of the divine glory of the newborn King in the miraculous virgin birth, in the song of the angelic choir, and in the wondrous star that guided the Wise Men. There also are numerous tokens of the coming of the one who was meek and lowly in heart. He was not born into the palaces and mansions of the high and mighty of the day, but he was born in a stable to a young peasant girl of true piety. His first visitors were the lowly shepherds from the hillsides.

One of our Christmas carols depicts Christ as the second Adam from above come to reinstate us in the divine love. He is truly the second Adam. The first Adam, although only a man, had aspired to be a god and had, thereby, provided an entry for sin and death into the world. The second Adam was the Son of God, but he willingly humbled himself and became a man in order to break the enslaving power of sin and death over the human race.

Paul's words set forth the mystery of the incarnation—God became flesh, the God-man. Human logic cannot resolve this essential paradox that in Jesus Christ the eternal God became a human being.

Some have seized on Paul's words in the first part of Philippians 2:7 as a clue. Literally Paul said of Christ, "He emptied himself." Some have taken this to mean that when Christ became a man, he emptied himself of his distinctly divine attributes. While this does preserve the truth that Jesus Christ was truly human, it does not accurately preserve the New Testament faith in one who was also our Lord and our God. Christ did not empty himself of deity when he became a man. Rather he exchanged the glorious status of Prince of heaven in order to be incarnate Son of God. When Paul wrote "emptied," he was not writing in the exact technical language of a precise theologian but in the poetic phrasing of a preacher painting a word picture of the Savior's descent from heaven to earth.

Some interpreters try to avoid the problem of "emptied" by interpreting verses 6-7 solely as a reference to Christ's earthly existence. That is, they rule out any reference to his preexistent glory in these verses. R. C. H. Lenski, for example, translates it this way: "He, who, existing in God's form, did not consider his being equal with God a thing of snatching but emptied himself in that he took slave's form when he got to be in man's likeness."[4] He interprets "a thing of snatching" as a desire for self-glorification. According to this view, the incarnate Christ, who was in the form of God as well as man, refused to follow the way of glorification that his divine status might rightfully have deserved. Instead he freely chose the way of humble service.

This may have been Paul's meaning; but as we have seen, the traditional interpretation need not mean that Christ "emptied" himself of deity when he became a human being. Indeed it cannot mean this and be consistent with other New Testament teachings.

The opposite error is equally false. Christ was truly human as well as truly divine. It is probably misleading to stress possible differences in word meanings in these verses. The words "form" and "likeness," for example, are often contrasted. The former means "essential likeness," and the latter means simply "likeness." However, if this line of thought is pressed too far, it can be argued that Christ was not a real man but only made in the likeness of a man. The result would be that we might fall into one of the oldest heresies of all—that which denies or depreciates the humanity of Jesus Christ. There were such people even in New Testament times who said that God did not really become a man; he only seemed to do so. Against such heresies the New Testament declares emphatically that the Word became flesh (John 1:14).

Without this incarnation there would be no gospel of salvation to preach. If Christ were only a man, he could not save us. We, therefore, believe the gospel portrait of one who had authority over nature, disease, demons, sin, and death. If Christ were only divine, he could not so share our plight as to deliver us from it. We, therefore, believe in one who got hungry, thirsty, and tired—one who was tempted as we are yet without sin.

Paul's use of the word "servant" reminds us that the mode of his incarnate life was one of service. Jesus himself said that he came not to be served but to serve others. Many of that day were expecting a messiah who would be a mighty monarch sitting on a royal throne or a great general riding a prancing white horse. Instead the true Messiah was one who engaged in lowly service to others.

Jesus clearly envisioned his mission in terms of service. When in his hometown synagogue at Nazareth, he was invited to read the Scripture lesson; he read from one of the servant passages of Isaiah these words:

" 'The Spirit of the Lord is upon me,
    because he has anointed me to preach good news to the poor.
    He has sent me to proclaim release to the captives
    and recovering of sight to the blind,
    to set at liberty those who are oppressed,
    to proclaim the acceptable year of the Lord.' "

Luke 4:18-19

Then he told the assembly, " 'Today this scripture has been fulfilled in your hearing' " (Luke 4:21).

As Peter later said in summarizing the ministry of Jesus, he "went about doing good" (Acts 10:38). He, however, was not that kind of "do-gooder" who gets some selfish satisfaction out of doing an occasional good turn for people whom he thinks of as "needy cases." There were many people in need all about Jesus, but he considered them as people, not "cases." True compassion moved him to seek out the sick, the sorrowing, and the sinful. When he, tired and weary, withdrew seeking needed rest, and the people followed, Jesus ministered to them with compassion and without complaint.

After eating the Last Supper with his disciples, Jesus arose from his place and proceeded to wash the disciples' feet. It was perhaps because this humble task was usually assigned to the person of lowest rank that none of the twelve had already washed the feet of the others. At any rate, the sight of their Lord and Master down on his knees with a towel and basin of water washing their feet must have made a profound impression on the disciples. In what better way could he have demonstrated that he came not to be served but to serve others?

The fulfillment of this ministry of service was the cross. This is the point in Philippians 2:8: "And being found in human form he humbled himself and became obedient unto death, even death on a cross."

Paul here portrays the cross as the deepest depth to which the eternal Christ descended for the redemption of sinful humanity. The apostle has shown how the Son of God stepped down from his royal throne in eternal glory to become a man. He has reminded us that this incarnate life was one of humble service to others in the name of God. Now he points out how Christ humbled himself by becoming obedient to death; and this death, Paul exclaims, was the death of the cross! Crucifixion was one of the worst possible deaths ever devised by the malicious minds of sinful men. Modern methods of execution are humane by comparison, for crucifixion was designed not merely to execute but to degrade and torture the victim.

That the Son of God should ever end up on a Roman cross is inconceivable by human standards. This is the reason the disciples could not bring themselves to believe Jesus when he told them of the coming cross, and it is the reason they saw the crucifixion at the time of his death as a crushing defeat. This is also the reason that the preaching of the cross was a stumbling block to many of their fellow-Jews. That God would allow his Anointed One to be so treated seemed unbelievable to minds trained to expect a messiah who would triumph over their enemies.

Also the message of the cross sounded like only much foolish talk to the non-Jewish world of the first century. Imagine how the message must have sounded to the ears of the cosmopolitan Romans in the time of Paul. To them Jesus was only a Jewish peasant, a carpenter who had turned religious teacher; after living and teaching in the eastern provinces for a few years, this Jesus had been arrested and executed as a criminal by the Roman Procurator Pontius Pilate. Then men like Paul dared to tell their hearers that this victim of the Roman cross was none other than the Son of God, the Savior of the world. To the Greeks and Romans this seemed utterly incredible, even ridiculous.

In this passage in Philippians Paul did not try to explain what led

Jesus Christ to such a death. He was writing to Christians, and he assumed they would understand. Thus he did not go into the death of Christ as the means of human redemption. He did write of Christ as *"obedient* unto death." Apparently this referred to his obedience to the will of his Father. Jesus saw himself as the Suffering Servant of Isaiah 53. The Servant suffered according to the will of God and on behalf of sinners.

Mark 10:45 is a good parallel to Philippians 2:8. The disciples had been wrangling about places of special honor in the kingdom (probably much the same spirit as was in the Philippian church). Jesus patiently tried to teach them that true greatness is measured in terms of humble self-giving service (this also was Paul's theme in Philippians 2:1-4). Jesus summed it up by saying: " 'For the Son of man also came not to be served but to serve, and to give his life as a ransom for many.' "

The Exaltation of Jesus as Lord (2:9-11)

Christ's followers did not see the glory of the cross at the time it happened. Jesus had taught and exemplified the way of self-giving love, but they did not understand. Their own religious expectations had been so influenced by worldly values that they missed his point. The same presuppositions caused them to see in the cross only a dark tragedy. However, the resurrection forced them to see Christ's life and death through different eyes. The resurrection showed that the way of self-giving love, even unto the cross, is God's way.

Verses 9-11 do not mention the resurrection as such. Rather Paul focused on the theme of Christ's exaltation, of which the resurrection was only the first phase. On the day of Pentecost when Peter preached to the people of Jerusalem, he focused on the resurrection; but he also referred to Christ's exaltation to God's right hand. He quoted a psalm of messianic kingship, Psalm 110:1. Then he said: " 'Let all the house of Israel therefore know assuredly that God has made him both Lord and Christ, this Jesus whom you crucified' " (Acts 2:36).

In the Ephesian letter Paul wrote of what God "accomplished in

Christ when he raised him from the dead and made him sit at his right hand in the heavenly places, far above all rule and authority and power and dominion, and above every name that is named, not only in this age but also in that which is to come; and he has put all things under his feet and has made him head over all things for the church, which is his body, the fulness of him who fills all in all" (Eph. 1:20-23).

Paul's words in Philippians 2:9-11 echo the same theme: "Therefore God has highly exalted him and bestowed on him the name which is above every name, that at the name of Jesus every knee should bow, in heaven and on earth and under the earth, and every tongue confess that Jesus Christ is Lord, to the glory of God the Father."

Paul may have had Isaiah 45:23 in mind as a background. This passage is a prophecy of universal acknowledgment of the sovereignty of God as Savior. Isaiah 45:23 says: " 'To me every knee shall bow, every tongue shall swear.' "

F. W. Beare says of Philippians 2:9-11 in relation to Isaiah 45:23: "This hymn affirms that this promise of world-wide acknowledgement of the saving sovereignty of God has been fulfilled in the exaltation of Christ."[5]

How are we to understand this description of universal acknowledgement of divine sovereignty? Frank Stagg says that it "may look two ways. It may reflect the divine offer of redemption to all God's creation. It more likely means that God's kingdom will be absolute in that the lordship of Christ must eventually be acknowledged everywhere."[6]

In other words, the passage does not promise universal salvation, which would call for voluntary universal acceptance. Rather this passage speaks of that which is not dependent on voluntary human response—the reality of God's sovereignty. God reigns. He always has reigned, but now in Christ his sovereign reign has been declared even more fully. Eventually, all of creation will be confronted with and acknowledge, however grudgingly, this divine sovereignty.

Revelation 5 is another good passage to read in connection with the study of Paul's hymn exalting Christ. This chapter contains the vision of the scroll sealed with seven seals that no man was worthy to open except the Lamb of God. When the Lamb stepped forward to take the sealed scroll, all of heaven was filled with songs of praise to him who was worthy to loose the seals because of his redemptive work on the cross. Then an angelic chorus sang, "Worthy is the Lamb who was slain, to receive power and wealth and wisdom and might and honor and glory and blessing!" (Rev. 5:12). Then these were joined by the voices of every creature in heaven, on earth, and under the earth singing, "To him who sits upon the throne and to the Lamb be blessing and honor and glory and might for ever and ever!" (Rev. 5:13).

"Every knee should bow. . . and every tongue confess that Jesus Christ is Lord, to the glory of God the Father." We cannot speak for the creatures in heaven or under the earth, but human beings should bow the knee before Jesus Christ and confess him as Lord.

One of the most moving portraits of the Son of God is Stenberg's "Crucifixion." It is said that the artist used a small girl as his consultant in the preliminary work on this painting. When he had finished the first sketch of the face of Jesus, the artist showed it to his landlady's little daughter and asked who she thought it was. The girl looked at it and said, "It is a good man." Knowing that he had failed, the artist tore up that sketch and began another. When it was complete, he asked her the same question as before. This time the child said that she thought it was a great sufferer. Again Stenberg destroyed his sketch and began another. It was a labor of love he performed on the third sketch, for when the child saw it she exclaimed, "It is the Lord!"

Anyone who looks at the portrait of Jesus painted with words by the writers of the New Testament will see the same Lord. If he dares to face the plain facts of gospel truth in this picture of Jesus with an open mind and heart, how can anyone fail to respond as did the girl, "It is the Lord!"

This is apparently what Thomas felt on that evening when he first saw the risen Christ. Thomas had been absent at the time Jesus had appeared to the other disciples. When they told Thomas what they had seen, the doubting disciple refused to believe. He demanded absolute proof by saying that unless he saw and felt the nail prints in the Savior's hands and put his hand into the spear thrust in his side, he would not believe. Then suddenly there was the risen Christ before him challenging Thomas to do just what he had said he must do in order to believe. The recorded response of Thomas was, "My Lord and my God" (John 20:28). We are not told what posture Thomas assumed as he spoke these words, but I cannot help but believe that he was on his knees.

It may sound mundane to be reminded again that Paul's great hymn of the exalted Christ grew out of his exhortation in Philippians 2:5, but it is true. He had been exhorting the Philippian believers, you remember, to display that sort of humility which characterized true Christian fellowship. His concern about the undercurrent of pride and faction at Philippi led the apostle to say, "Have this mind among yourselves, which is yours in Christ Jesus." Then follows this great hymn of the humble descent and exalted ascent of Christ.

Someone may wonder what this poetic description of Christ has to do with the problem of disunity in a church, and the very fact that we do wonder points up our sin of separating doctrine from actual living. We place the doctrine and worship of Christ on an exalted, spiritual plane; but we fail to see what this matter of the Spirit has to do with the way we live. Actually it has everything to do with the way we live if we are Christians.

The same painting of the crucifixion by Stenberg to which reference has already been made was hung in the gallery at Dusseldorf after its completion. Beneath it was this inscription: "This I did for thee; what hast thou done for me?" One day a young German aristocrat paused before the painting. He was moved by the artist's depiction of the sacrifice of Christ, and he was challenged by the inscription. The result was all the noble missionary work of the Moravians, inspired by their leader Count Nicholas von Zinzendorf.

5

Christ's Expendables

Philippians 2:12-30

During the early years of World War II W. L. White wrote a book entitled *They Were Expendable.*[1] The book is an account of the heroic exploits of a handful of American P T boat crews who fought a delaying action against the initial onslaught of the Japanese attack in the Philippines. Although they were hopelessly outnumbered by the enemy forces, these sailors risked all they had in a gallant struggle. Many of them, in fact, gave all they had to give—their lives. Since the dictionary defines "expendable" as "supplies or personnel involved in a calculated risk," it is apparent that Mr. White chose a very appropriate title for his book.

Shortly after the war Dr. Charles Maddry, a former Executive Secretary of the Southern Baptist Foreign Mission Board, published a book entitled *Christ's Expendables.*[2] His book consists of a number of short stories relating to the sacrificial endeavors of foreign missionary heroes and heroines. The men and women of whom Dr. Maddry wrote were truly expendable for Christ's sake. They were willing to spend and to be spent in order to share the gospel with a lost world. They, no less than the crews of the P T boats, were involved voluntarily in a great calculated risk, in which they stood to lose all.

In Philippians 2:12-30 the apostle Paul recorded his own narrative of "Christ's expendables." Paul, you remember, had been warning the Philippians about the dangers of dissension; and he had urged upon them the true spirit of Christian togetherness. The key to such real fellowship is that kind of genuine *agape* which is best exemplified in Jesus Christ our Lord. Paul, therefore, had urged his readers to share the mind of Christ. What he says in the verses before us now is not unrelated to all of this.

First, he followed up on earlier exhortations with another direct appeal for action by the Philippians (2:12-18). In that context he referred to his own willingness to give his life if necessary (2:17-18). Then he told of his plans to send Timothy to Philippi as soon as possible (2:19-24) and to send Epaphroditus right away (2:25-28).

At first glance it may seem that Paul was merely following up his exhortation by sharing some personal plans and hopes with regard to himself, Timothy, and Epaphroditus. A more careful reading, however, seems to indicate that Paul was attempting to illustrate the mind of Christ in terms of these three lives. He had shown how Christ was expendable for our sakes; then in these verses he sought to show how he, Timothy, and Epaphroditus were expendable for Christ's sake. He was apparently trying to challenge the Philippians, thereby, to show the same kind of self-forgetful devotion to the Lord.

Paul did not spell this out by saying "Follow our example," but one does not have to read between the lines to get this message. Of himself he said that he was ready to be poured out as a sacrificial offering if need be. Timothy was described as a man who placed the highest priority on the Lord's business. Epaphroditus was one who risked his very life for the work of Christ.

Working Out Your Salvation (2:12-13)

Few verses have been so misunderstood as Philippians 2:12, "Work out your own salvation with fear and trembling." These words have been cited by some as proof that Christianity is not an evangelical religion calling for sinners to be born again but a commonsense approach to moral living available to all people of good will. These words also have been quoted by modern Pharisees intent on proving that people merit the favor of God by their good works.

As a *proof-text* these words are admirably suited for such

purposes. However, when these words are studied as part of what Paul wrote to the Philippians, they lose their effectiveness as a proof-text. A key principle of serious biblical interpretation calls for a verse to be studied in context. Philippians 2:12 is an excellent illustration of the need for this principle.

First of all, this verse is part of a letter to Christians in a church, not an evangelistic appeal to unbelievers. The apostle, therefore, assumed that his readers had already experienced the saving grace of God. He would never have advised an unbeliever to work out his own salvation. Picture the scene at the jail at Philippi. The terrified jailer asks, " 'What must I do to be saved?' " (Acts 16:30). Can you imagine Paul answering, "Work out your own salvation with fear and trembling"?

A consideration of context includes the connection between Philippians 2:12 and the verses preceding it. A key word here is "obeyed." Paul had been calling the Philippians to genuine unity (1:27) based on self-giving love (2:1-4). This way, Paul had written, is the essence of Christ's way, which believers should share (2:5-11). The central feature of this way was Christ's death, of which Paul wrote that he "became obedient unto death, even death on a cross" (2:8). Notice the word "obedient." Christ gave himself in this way of self-giving love in obedience to the Father's will. Paul's point in 2:12 is that the Philippians who have always obeyed in the past should continue in this way.

Take special note also of the close connection between verses 12 and 13: "Therefore, my beloved, as you have always obeyed, so now, not only as in my presence but much more in my absence, work out your own salvation with fear and trembling; for God is at work in you, both to will and to work for his good pleasure." Even a casual reader would be struck by the seeming contradiction between verse 12 and verse 13. In one verse Paul wrote as if the entire enterprise rested on the Philippians; yet in the next he wrote as if all depended on God.

This is not a contradiction, but a paradox. Although these two statements are logically inconsistent, Paul's two truths are both valid. The doctrine of grace in a sense does teach that everything ultimately depends on God. Yet God's grace is never substituted for human effort; rather grace calls forth the best and most vigorous human efforts.

Thus Paul's appeal to bring their salvation to completion with fear and trembling was set in the context of God's gracious and adequate motivating and energizing toward the same goal.

This same paradox of grace and works is stated in Ephesians 2:8-10. Verses 8-9 are far more familiar to evangelicals than verse 10. The gospel of saving grace for sinners is nowhere stated more clearly: "For by grace you have been saved through faith; and this is not your own doing, it is the gift of God—not because of works, lest any man should boast." Yet Paul immediately added these words: "For we are his workmanship, created in Christ Jesus for good works."

Paul did not write a systematic study of salvation. However, when all of Paul's references to salvation are studied, it appears that he wrote of salvation sometimes as a past event, sometimes as a present experience, and sometimes as a future hope.[3] In Philippians 2:12 he was writing of the continuation of salvation as a present experience. His words in verse 13 remind us that God's grace and power continue to be the basis for salvation. It is incorrect to say that God's grace operates in the initial phase of salvation but human works operate in the later stages, for the God of grace is at work from beginning to end.

The words "fear and trembling" should be understood in this context. F. W. Beare writes: "Such fear and trembling is not caused by apprehension that God may turn against them at the last, that their hope of salvation is really precarious and insecure. It is prompted rather by the sense that it is *God* with whom they have to do, that they are constantly in his presence, that he is acting effectively among them and within them."[4]

Thus the very sense of God's gracious presence with them keeps taut the tension between what they are and what God would have them to be.

The opposite of vigorously pressing on toward the completion of

God's saving purpose is a kind of moral complacency and spiritual lethargy. Later in the letter Paul spelled out his own stance as that of a pilgrim ever pressing on, not as a person who believed he already had arrived (3:12-14). Apparently there was in Philippi a tendency toward complacency and its accompanying ills—moral confusion and disruptive dissension. Over against these Paul wrote the exhortation in verses 12-13.

Shining as Lights in a Dark World (2:14-16)

Verses 14-16 add further support to this view. Moral confusion and disruptive dissension are dangers against which Paul warned: "Do all things without grumbling or questioning, that you may be blameless and innocent, children of God without blemish in the midst of a crooked and perverse generation, among whom you shine as lights in the world, holding fast the word of life, so that in the day of Christ I may be proud that I did not run in vain or labor in vain."

Beare believes that when Paul wrote verses 12-18, he had in mind Moses' farewell charge recorded in Deuteronomy 32:1-5. Paul like Moses in Moab faced the prospect of death. Paul had been with the Philippians in the past, but now he was absent from them. Like Israel after Moses' death, the Philippians must press on toward God's purpose for them without their former leader. But what was important was that God was with them.

The clearest parallel in wording is between Deuteronomy 32:5 and Philippians 2:15. However, Paul used these words in a different way than Moses did. Moses traced the sinful history of Israel and rebuked them. Paul assumed that pagan society, not the believers, was crooked and perverse. Paul expected the church in Philippi to be like light in the darkness.

Paul affirmed the best as his hope for the Philippians, but his words imply all was not well with them. The words "grumbling" and "questioning" ("murmurings and disputings," KJV) are found repeatedly in the Old Testament account of Israel's wilderness wanderings. (See Ex. 16:7-8; Num. 11:1.) The strong implication is that the Philippians needed to heed this warning. Otherwise why would Paul make such a strong plea for *koinonia* (1:27; 2:1-2) based on humble, self-giving love (2:3-4)? His warning in 4:2-3 shows that there was some murmuring and dissension in the Philippian church.

Yet the tone of Paul's exhortation is basically positive and hopeful. There is a noticeable difference between the tone in Philippians and in 1 Corinthians. When Paul warned the Corinthians about dissension, he was much more direct. In 1 Corinthians 10:16-11 he drew a series of parallels between the Corinthians and Israel's wilderness sins. In verse 10 he warned the Corinthians not to grumble and reminded them that some of the Israelites perished because of this same sin.

How account for this difference in tone? One factor apparently was that the problem in Philippians was not so deep or widespread as at Corinth. Another factor may have been Paul's special closeness to the Philippians. Perhaps Paul also felt that an affirming tone would be more effective in dealing with the Philippians.

Whatever the reason, the apostle obviously expected them to move beyond their grumblings and disputes. He expected them to be light-bearers in a dark world, "holding fast" or "holding forth the word of life" (KJV). The word may be translated either way. Since both ideas fit the context, it is difficult to rule out either as a possible meaning.

Perhaps Paul had in mind the saying of Jesus recorded in Matthew 5:16: " 'Let your light so shine before men, that they may see your good works and give glory to your Father who is in heaven.' "

The last part of verse 16 shows that Paul's own feelings were deeply involved in the life of the Philippian church. To see them united in Christian love and reflecting Christ's light in a dark world would cause Paul to know he had not lived in vain.

Paul was like a father who is anxious about some tendencies he sees in his children. He gives them a mild but serious warning, while at the same time he affirms their potential for good. He tells them what he expects of them, and he reminds them how he will burst with fatherly pride when they fulfill his expectations.

Willing to Give All in Sacrificial Service (2:17-18)

Paul's personal commitment becomes even clearer in verses 17-18: "Even if I am to be poured out as a libation upon the sacrificial offering of your faith, I am glad and rejoice with you all. Likewise you also should be glad and rejoice with me."

Paul used an analogy from the area of sacrificial offerings. Commentators debate whether Paul had in mind a Jewish or pagan sacrificial system. They also debate such questions as: Who is the priest in the analogy? What is the sacrifice?

Here is J. B. Lightfoot's interpretation of the analogy: "The Philippians are the priests; their faith (or their good works springing from their faith) is the sacrifice: St. Paul's life-blood the accompanying libation."[5] A libation was a drink offering poured out in connection with the offering of a victim on the altar.

The Philippians then are seen as priests and sacrifice. This is consistent with Romans 12:1 where Paul challenged Christians to present their bodies as living sacrifices. To describe his highest expectations for the Philippians Paul turned from the analogy of light in verses 15-16 to the analogy of sacrificial offerings in verse 17. Paul expected them to give themselves unselfishly and sacrificially for the cause of Christ.

That is the crux of his appeal to this point. He spelled it out in 2:3-4 and proclaimed it as the Christian way in 2:5-11. Rather than acting from selfish pride they were to put others first. Like Christ they were to give of themselves, if need be even unto death.

Paul had already stated his own attitude about life and death in 1:19-26. He was aware that he might be called on to lay down his life. Or God might have more work for him to do. In either case, Paul was ready. His statement in 2:17 is an additional statement of his willingness to give his life if need be.

The Greek words for "rejoice" and "rejoice together with" are used in verse 17 to express Paul's attitude toward this possible total sacrifice. Paul used the same words of what he trusted would be the Philippians' response to the mingling of their lives with Paul's in sacrificial service. Martin observes: "The piling up of terms for 'joy'

. . . are characteristic of this letter as a whole. They underline Paul's indominable spirit under trial and express the confidence that his readers will catch the spirit too."[6]

There are two pictures on the seal of the American Baptist Foreign Mission Society. On one side is an ox standing beside a plow, and on the other side is an altar. The inscription beneath the pictures reads, "Ready for Either." This sums up Paul's outlook and what should be the normal Christian outlook.

This is the positive ideal in the doctrine of the priesthood of all believers. Too many think of this basic Protestant belief in negative terms. We are quick to point out that we need no sacramental system of priests as mediators between ourselves and God. Jesus is our Great High Priest who made the supreme sacrifice for our sins by offering himself. What we sometimes fail to perceive is that each believer is in one sense a priest offering up sacrifices unto God. It is not primarily the placing of a portion of our possessions at the Lord's disposal, but it is first of all offering ourselves unto the Lord (2 Cor. 8:5; see Rom. 12:1).

Is not this what Jesus meant by "taking up the cross" and by "losing your life for the sake of the gospel"? He meant that we must make the basic sacrifice of placing all that we have and are at his disposal.

When we compare ourselves with Paul and others of Christ's expendables, we readily see that many of us know little of what real sacrifice is. We read about sacrifice, and we sing about sacrifice; sometimes we even dare to apply the term to something we have done. It usually proves true, however, that the people who do the most talking about sacrifice know the least of what it really means.

This is not to say that there are not men and women who share the Spirit of Christ to the degree that their whole life is a sacrifice for Christ's sake; it is to say that these people stand so close to the cross that they are too aware of the sacrifice of Christ to be aware of their own.

David Livingstone, the missionary doctor and explorer, who literally opened the dark continent of Africa to the gospel, made as many sacrifices as any man since Paul. He left home and native land for the privations in a jungle of ignorance, disease, and iniquity. He expended blood, sweat, and tears in offering his life for Christ in Africa. Livingstone, however, wrote, "I never made a sacrifice. Of this we ought not to talk when we remember the great sacrifice which He made who left His Father's throne on high to give Himself for us."[7] Real sacrifice is living in the light of and in the power of the cross.

Putting God and Others First (2:19-24)

Paul turned from direct exhortation (2:12-18) to tell of his plans to send Timothy to Philippi as soon as possible (2:19-24). However, Paul had a twofold purpose in this part of the letter. On the surface he informed them of his plans to send Timothy and hopefully to come himself. Yet the way in which the apostle described Timothy provided the Philippians with another flesh-and-blood example of self-giving service.

Paul hoped to send Timothy to them as soon as possible. How soon? Paul said, "I hope therefore to send him just as soon as I see how it will go with me" (v. 23). Apparently Paul needed Timothy until his own fate became clear. He hoped the outcome of his trial was near. When the outcome was known, he would send Timothy.

Verse 24 is often quoted as indicating that Paul expected a favorable outcome. He wrote, "I trust in the Lord that shortly I myself shall come also." This verse needs to be set alongside other verses in the letter in which Paul spoke of his own view of his fate: 1:19-26; 2:17. Apparently he did not yet rule out the possibility of conviction and even execution, but he remained hopeful of being acquitted.

He intended to send Timothy, Paul wrote, "so that I may be cheered by news of you" (2:19). Paul hoped that his letter, which would arrive before Timothy, would be used by God to help the Philippians begin to move toward the ideal set forth in the letter. He also expected Timothy to be his representative in Philippi and to help them move even further toward the goal of Christian unity based on self-giving love. Thus he hoped Timothy could report news that would cheer his heart.

The Philippians already knew Timothy. He had been there before. The book of Acts lists Timothy among those who were with Paul in his first visit to Philippi (16:3; 17:14). Paul wrote, "Timothy's worth you know, how as a son with a father he has served with me in the gospel" (Phil. 2:22).

The heart of Philippians 2:19-24 are verses 20-21, where Paul said of Timothy: "I have no one like him, who will be genuinely anxious for your welfare. They all look after their own interests, not those of Jesus Christ."

The word translated "like" means "of like mind or soul." The word "him" is added by the translators on the assumption that Paul meant, "I have no one else with me who is of like mind to Timothy." Other translators assume Paul meant that he had no one of such like mind to Paul himself: "There is no one else here who sees things as I do" (NEB).

Either way, we cannot but wonder what this says about the state of Christian commitment where Paul was. The most pessimistic view would be that no other believer near Paul shared Paul's concern for the Philippians because all were more concerned about their own affairs than about the work of Christ.

This probably was not Paul's meaning. Earlier in the letter Paul had spoken of some believers who were acting out of envy and strife; however he also spoke of others who preached Christ out of love and good will (1:15-18). Therefore, at least some of the Christians were seeking sincerely to serve Christ.

In 2:21 Paul probably had reference to his own helpers, not to Christians in the area; and his point was that no one was so well-suited for this mission as Timothy. This does not necessarily mean that all Paul's helpers were complacent and selfish. If Paul wrote from Rome, Luke was with him at least part of the time. He surely was not unconcerned with the work of Christ. Some of Paul's helpers may have been involved in other missions; and others probably were involved in personal, family, and vocational concerns.

Timothy had the background and commitment for this mission. He knew the Philippians, and they knew him. He was close to Paul and shared the apostle's goals for and love for the Philippians. He had proven himself on many similar missions. He also was willing to make this his number one priority. The mission to Philippi would take time and effort. Timothy was willing to put this concern before other more personal concerns.

This kind of putting first things first was and is too rare. We have said that Paul probably did not mean to issue a strong condemnation against the Christian community near him or against his more immediate helpers. In other words, we need to qualify verse 21. However, we must beware watering it down. Unfortunately, preoccupation with our own interests and concerns is a besetting sin for Christians in every generation.

This was a basic problem in Philippi. Paul warned about a selfish pride that focused on selfish interests (2:3). Over against this he said, "Let each of you look not only to his own interests, but also to the interests of others" (2:4). This was what Timothy did. He did not put his own personal concerns first. Instead he put first the needs of the Philippians. This was not because Timothy had no personal concerns and affairs to manage. He did. But he put the cause of Christ and the needs of others before his own interests, needs, and concerns.

The Patriots is a play by Sidney Kingsley. *The Patriots* were Thomas Jefferson and Alexander Hamilton, who each in his own distinctive way was completely dedicated to the noble experiment of American freedom. The drama centers around the strong political rivalry between Jefferson and Hamilton. Seldom did they see eye to eye politically. Hamilton suspected the Virginian of being a rabble-rouser who wanted a revolution along the pattern of the one in France. Jefferson feared Hamilton's alliance with the moneyed aristocracy of the land.

The climax of the play is a tense scene in which Hamilton pledges to see that the Jefferson-Burr deadlock for president is decided in Jefferson's favor. This would involve sacrifices for both. Jefferson was tired of politics and yearned to retire to his beloved Monticello. Hamilton disagreed with the politics of Jefferson, but he knew the

Virginian was honest. He knew that his action would arouse the temper of the conniving scoundrel Aaron Burr, whom he suspected of planning to assume dictatorial powers, were he elected. This would mean a duel with Burr, who was a crack shot. Hamilton knew this would be disastrous for him, as indeed it was.

This drama illustrates a quality which true patriotism and true religion have in common—the willingness to be completely involved in a cause far larger than any individual. How this note needs to be sounded throughout the land today! We have lived by the philosophy of "what's in it for me?" We do indeed need to ask not what our nation can do for us but what we can do for our nation.

This same challenge also needs to be heard among the slumbering forces of Christendom. There are too many summer soldiers and sunshine patriots among the ranks of church people, members who shrink from every challenge and flee before every difficulty; multitudes who have never risen to the challenge of a cause far more important than anything they have or are.

Timothy was the exception rather than the rule in his total involvement in the cause of Christ. Most people are so completely absorbed in their own affairs that they have no time nor interest for God's work or the needs of others. They are so busy building their own petty kingdoms that the eternal kingdom of God occupies only passing or peripheral interest for them. The Bible uses the words "first" and "all" to describe a believer's relation to the Lord. We are to seek *first* God's kingdom and his righteousness, and we are to love the Lord with *all* our heart, mind, soul, and strength.

Risking All for Christ's Sake (2:25-30)

Paul deliberately chose Timothy to go to Philippi. He also deliberately reminded the Philippians of the kind of man Timothy was. Timothy, like Paul, was a flesh-and-blood example of a man committed to Jesus Christ and to his way of self-giving love. But Paul had yet another example of this spirit—one even better known to the Philippians than Timothy. Paul wrote of Epaphroditus in verses 25-30.

This passage is helpful in putting together the background to the

Philippian letter. Epaphroditus is mentioned only here and in Philippians 4:18. He had brought a gift from the Philippians (4:18), and he had come as their representative to help Paul ("your messenger and minister to my need," 2:25). While there, he had become ill and almost died. Word of this illness had reached Philippi, and Epaphroditus' distress was deepened by the knowledge that his friends were aware of his illness (2:26-27).

God had spared Epaphroditus, and Paul had decided to send him home. The wording seems to imply that Epaphroditus was the person who delivered the letter Paul wrote to the Philippians. Paul seems to have anticipated some of the Philippians objecting to Epaphroditus' return; they may have felt he should stay and continue to minister to Paul. At any rate Paul made it very clear that he had the highest possible regard for Epaphroditus and that it was Paul's idea to send him home. He referred to Epaphroditus as "my brother and fellow worker and fellow soldier" (2:25). He spoke of his own distress at Epaphroditus' illness and then said of his return: "I am the more eager to send him, therefore, that you may rejoice at seeing him again, and that I may be less anxious" (2:28).

Then he added this tribute to Epaphroditus: "So receive him in the Lord with all joy; and honor such men, for he nearly died for the work of Christ, risking his life to complete your service to me" (2:29-30).

The last part of verse 30 may sound like a slighting remark, as if the Philippians had only sent Paul part of what they should have sent and Epaphroditus had come to try to complete it. The King James Version, which is more literal at this point, makes it sound even worse. Epaphroditus came "to supply your lack of service toward me" (v. 30).

Vincent makes these helpful comments: "So far from implying a censure . . . that clause is a most delicate, courteous, and sympathetic tribute to both Epaphroditus and the Philippians. The gift to Paul was the gift of the church as a body. It was a sacrificial offering of love. What was lacking, and what would have been grateful to Paul and to the church alike, was the church's presentation of this offering in person. This was impossible, and Paul represents Epaphroditus as supplying this lack by his affectionate and zealous ministry."[8]

E. F. Scott points out that Paul meant "that there was only one thing wanting in the kindness the Philippians had shown him, and that was their own presence. This was what he most desired; and since they could not give it, Epaphroditus had made up for the want."[9]

The key word in verses 29-30 is the word translated "risking." The word means to expose to risk or danger. At times it was used of gambling. Lightfoot translates this "having gambled with his own life." The same idea but not the same word was used in Romans 16:4 where Paul said of Priscilla and Aquila that they "risked their necks for my life."

Epaphroditus had undertaken a mission that was fraught with dangers. The stakes were his life. In this sense he risked his life. His life was precious to him, but he risked it for something more precious—the work of Christ seen in his church's ministry to Paul. As it turned out, he did almost lose his life.

Like Christ in Paul's hymn Christians are not to grasp their own rights and privileges but to give of themselves in humble love to and for others. Christ risked his life and gave his life.

"Paul does not explicitly hold up Epaphroditus' self-abnegation and sacrificial service as an example to the Philippians, but the suggestion is easily implied. How can they persist in their divisive quarreling in the presence of one of their own who gambled his very life in his devotion to both Paul and his own church?"[10]

There was a group in Christian history who were called *parabolani*, a name taken from the word used by Paul of Epaphroditus. This was a voluntary brotherhood who risked their lives by performing various hazardous acts of service. Charles Kingsley in his novel *Hypatia* describes the *parabolani* as ministering in the slums of fifth-century Alexandria by "carrying food and clothing, helping sick to the hospital, and dead to the burial; cleaning out the infected houses—for the fever was all but perennial in those quarters—and comforting the dying with good news of forgiveness from above."[11]

As I was writing this chapter, news came of the death of Archie Dunaway. Archie and his wife Margaret had served most of their adult lives in Africa, first in Nigeria and then in Rhodesia. He gave his life to Christ long ago and offered it afresh to him each day. He gave his time, his energy, his talents, and his life. He was slain as one of many victims of the senseless, brutal violence that haunts our world. He knew his work involved an element of risk, but he took the risk for Christ's sake. Christ had called him to be one of his ambassadors; to Africa he went, in Africa he stayed, and there he died.

6

Life Turned Inside Out

Philippians 3:1-11

When a famous person claims to have experienced a religious conversion, the news media generally play it up. Often the reports have subtle overtones that cast doubt on the validity and permanence of the experience. Sometimes later events in the person's life seem to justify such initial skepticism; often, however, the convert becomes a different kind of person.

Saul of Tarsus was a famous person. His conversion to Christianity caused a great stir. The amazing news was that a persecutor of Christians now professed to be a Christian. No doubt the initial reports of Saul's conversion were heard with much skepticism—by non-Christians and by many Christians. But subsequent events leave no doubt about Saul's conversion.

The book of Acts records the events related to Saul's encounter with Christ. References in Paul's letters give added insight into the significance and meaning of his conversion. Philippians 3:1-11 is such a passage. In this passage Paul shows how he viewed his old life before and after his conversion. He also shows the new goals and values of his life in Christ.

This passage is valuable in distinguishing what should be normative in all conversions from what was unique in Paul's. Much confusion results when we fail to define what are the basic characteristics of true conversion. The circumstances and feelings in individual conversions differ, but the basic reality is the same.

William James gave this classic definition of conversion: "The process, gradual or sudden, by which a self hitherto divided, and consciously wrong inferior and unhappy, becomes unified consciously right, superior and happy, in consequence of its firmer hold upon religious realities."[1]

William Barclay entitled his study of Christian conversion *Turning to God.* He sees the essence of conversion as the "turning of a man's mind and heart and life in the direction of God."[2] He further describes this as a *turning from* old ways of thinking and acting and a *turning to* a new life-style growing out of a personal relation with God in Christ.

The Bible uses several analogies to express this reality, but all these analogies stress the newness of the convert. He is born anew spiritually in a way comparable to a newborn child. He is a new moral and spiritual creation comparable to the miracle of God's original creation of heaven and earth. He is like a person who has taken off old, dirty clothes and put on new, clean ones.

After Augustine was converted, he was seen at a distance by one of his former companions, who called out, "Augustine, it is I." The new convert called back, "It is no longer I." He was echoing Paul's words from Galatians 2:20, "It is no longer I who live, but Christ who lives in me."

The convert is like a new and different person. The more obvious and extreme were the person's sins—Paul's persecution and Augustine's immorality—the more obvious to observers are the changes. Life has been turned inside out; the convert sees things differently and lives life differently—so much so that he may not even seem like the same person.

But paradoxically, the person is never more himself than when he is converted. His identity is not lost; rather it is found. He begins to become the distinct personality God intends him to be. Paul became a new person, but he was still Paul. The same kind of zeal with which he once persecuted the church he now directed toward advancing the cause of Christ. The keen intellect of Augustine, which had once sent him searching for answers among the world's philosophies, now was harnessed for Christ. As a result, the theological insights of Augustine have been read and pondered for fifteen centuries.

An Abrupt Warning (3:1-2)

Most translations of chapter 3 sound as if Paul was about to conclude the letter: "Finally, my brethren, rejoice in the Lord. To write the same things to you is not irksome to me, and is safe to you" (3:1). The first word is found also in 4:8. It can mean "finally," but it also can mean "in addition." At times Paul used it as a conclusion (2 Cor. 13:11). At other times he used it more as a transition (1 Thess. 4:1; 2 Thess. 3:1).

What did Paul mean by "the same things" in the last part of verse 1? One possibility is that he was referring to some theme repeated several times in the Philippian letter. If so, he could have been referring to his repeated emphasis on rejoicing in the Lord (2:18,28; 3:1; 4:4). Or he could have had in mind the warnings against dissension and the corresponding challenges to unity based on unselfish commitment (1:27; 2:1-5,14,17,20-21,30; 4:1-3).

Another possible meaning of "the same things" is this: Paul may have meant something about which he had earlier written or spoken to the Philippians. Thus the repetition may refer not to repetition within this letter but to some theme made familiar from Paul's earlier communications with the Philippians. For example, the abrupt warning in verse 2 may have been a warning Paul already had given to the Philippians. If so, Paul was saying that repeating this stern warning was not irksome to him because the warning was aimed at their safety and well-being.

The reader experiences a kind of jolt in passing from 3:1 to 3:2. In verse 1 Paul is saying "rejoice in the Lord." Then suddenly he says, "Look out for the dogs, look out for the evil-workers, look out for those who mutilate the flesh" (3:2). Not only does the subject change but also the tone. The tone in verse 2 is as harsh as anything Paul wrote in Galatians or in 2 Corinthians 10-13.

Some scholars feel driven to the conclusion that 3:2 was not part of the same letter. F. W. Beare, for example, considers 3:2-21 as a part of another Pauline letter to Philippi. Somehow this part of the other letter ended up in this final edition of Philippians. Beare bases his conclusion on "the seriousness of the break and the complete lack of connection between this chapter and the remainder of the letter."[3]

Those scholars who defend the unity of Philippians make two points: For one thing, as E. F. Scott points out: "Paul is not writing a studied essay, but a letter in which his mind moves freely. Something has occurred to him which he has overlooked, and now he hastens to set it down."[4]

But the strongest defense of the letter's unity is that the themes in chapter 3:2-21 are in other chapters of the letter. E. F. Scott is emphatic in saying that this chapter "connects so closely with the others that the epistle would be incomplete without it."[5] There is continuity and discontinuity between 3:2-21 and the rest of the letter. On one hand, Paul introduced a new subject; on the other hand, the subject and how Paul dealt with it have connections with other chapters.

Frank Stagg writes: "Emphasis upon the importance of being right 'minded' (3:15), upon 'example' (3:17), upon 'suffering' (3:10), and upon the 'cross of Christ' (3:18) is the strongest kind of internal evidence that chapter 3 is continuous with chapter 2."[6]

A strong emphasis on Christian maturity runs through chapter 3. This blends smoothly into the contents of chapter 4.

Who were the "evil-workers" mentioned in verse 2? They obviously were some group stressing circumcision and righteousness according to the Jewish law. They may have been non-Christian Jews; but more likely they were Judaizers, Jews who professed faith in Jesus as Messiah but who insisted on circumcision and legal righteousness (Acts 15:1). Paul had done battle with them many times. They seem to have followed Paul's missionary trail and spent their time confusing the Gentile converts.

There were few Jews in Philippi during Paul's initial visit, not even enough for a synagogue. Still it is unlikely that the Judaizers would completely bypass Philippi. Paul's Galatian letter reflects Paul's agitation at their inroads in the Galatian churches. Most of the Galatian letter is devoted to this problem. By comparison the Judaizers receive only passing attention in the Philippian letter. Apparently the problem was not so real or so pressing as in Galatia. Paul used strong language in Philippians 3:2, but he quickly moved to a more positive theme—his new life in Christ.

A Drastic Change (3:3-7)

The matter over which Paul fought the Judaizers is no longer an issue, but the principle is as enduring as human history. That is, circumcision is no longer a religious battlefield; but this question is: "Do we have the ability to control our lives and destiny, or do we need God's grace and power working in and through us?"

This was Paul's understanding of the issue at stake. Paul's opponents probably would have argued that circumcision and the law are signs of God's grace at work in those who keep God's ordinances and laws.

By contrast, Paul wrote, "We are the true circumcision, who worship God in spirit, and glory in Christ Jesus, and put no confidence in the flesh" (3:3). According to Paul, circumcision originally was given to Abraham as a sign of his covenant relation with God, which was based on Abraham's faith response to God's grace. Therefore, Paul insisted that true circumcision is inward and spiritual (Rom. 2:28-29; Col. 2:11). The "circumcised" in the symbolic sense are those whose worship is a matter of the Spirit, not of ritual and letter of the law. They trust in and glory in Christ Jesus, not in themselves.

"Flesh" is another key word in the passage. Paul used the word differently than it is used today. To the man on the street "flesh" means that soft tissue which makes up a body. In modern religious usage "sins of the flesh" refer to sensual sins.

At times Paul used "flesh" to mean the literal fleshly part of the body, as when he referred to those "who mutilate the flesh" (Phil. 3:2). He also referred to works or sins of the flesh, although he included a wider range of sins than sensual sins (Gal. 5:19-21). This is because Paul's basic meaning for "flesh" is a way of life based on human rather than divine resources. Life in the Spirit or in Christ is the opposite of life in the flesh.

Our closest modern parallel to what Paul meant by life in the flesh is humanism. Secular humanism is the view that man can live out of purely human resources apart from any need for God.

As we have noted, Paul's Judaizing opponents would have violently disagreed with this analysis. They considered themselves deeply spiritual and devoutly religious people. Perhaps that was the reason Paul chose such an offensive description of the basis for their hope. Paul was insisting that in their preoccupation with heritage, rituals, and laws they were actually trusting in themselves, not in God.

At this point Paul spoke with the voice of experience. No one knew better than he what it meant to trust in heritage, rituals, and laws. Paul knew exactly how his opponents looked at life, because he once had shared their basic presuppositions. In fact, he had reached the highest level of attainment based on these presuppositions.

This was his point in verses 4-6. He had just described himself and other Christians as those who "put no confidence in the flesh" (3:3). Then he began to reflect on the past: "Though I myself have reason for confidence in the flesh also. If any other man thinks he has reason for confidence in the flesh, I have more" (3:4). Then Paul listed four aspects of his own rich Jewish heritage and three areas in which he had exercised his own choices.

His heritage was the highest and best: "circumcised on the eighth day, of the people of Israel, of the tribe of Benjamin, a Hebrew born of Hebrews" (3:5). Paul was circumcised on the eighth day as a descendant of Abraham through the line of promise (Gen. 17:12; Lev. 12:3). He bore proudly the covenant name Israel, given to Jacob and his descendants. He was not one of mixed blood but a pure Israelite, whose family had preserved their national and even their tribal identity. He was of the tribe of Benjamin, which along with Judah had remained loyal to the Davidic line. Although he was born in Tarsus outside the Holy Land (Acts 22:3), he and his family retained their knowledge of and use of their native language (Acts 21:40). This shows that although he grew up in a Greek culture, his family carefully preserved their Hebrew identity, culture, and language.

All of this was the heritage to which Paul had been born. What follows shows how completely Paul had committed himself to that heritage. He listed three areas of his own choices and attainments: "As to the law a Pharisee, as to zeal a persecutor of the church, as to the righteousness under the law blameless" (3:5-6).

Although born in Tarsus of Cilicia, he had studied in Jerusalem under Gamaliel (Acts 22:3), a noted Pharisee (Acts 5:34). At one of his hearings in Acts Paul said, " 'I am a Pharisee, a son of Pharisees' " (Acts 23:6). Conditioned as we are by the negative evaluation of Pharisaism in the Gospels, we may forget how the Pharisees were seen by most first-century Jews. Many viewed them as the best embodiment of the faith of Israel.

Some interpreters think Paul wrote with a touch of irony in Philippians 3:5-6. Paul the Christian surely saw the faults of Pharisaic Judaism. The larger passage hones in on its chief fault. However, in verses 5-6 Paul probably was describing how he felt about being a Pharisee at the time he was a Pharisee. He began his defense before Agrippa in a similar way, " 'According to the strictest party of our religion I have lived as a Pharisee' " (Acts 26:5).

When Paul was a Pharisee, he regarded his persecution of the church as a mark of his genuine zeal. None of us can read this without feeling how ironical this was: a good man in the name of God persecuting other believers in God to prison and to death (Acts 8:3; 9:1; 26:9-11). No one felt the irony so strongly as Paul did after his conversion. However, there was a time in his life when he and many of his associates saw Paul's actions as a mark of genuine religious fervor. Paul was so zealous that he was not content to try to stamp out Christianity in Jerusalem; he intended to stamp it out everywhere (Acts. 9:1-2; 26:11; Gal. 1:13).

Paul the Pharisee also thought he had successfully attained the status of being blameless so far as the law was concerned. In retrospect Paul saw how foolish this had been; he makes this plain in the remainder of Philippians 3. In the Philippian church there seem to have been those who believed they had attained perfection. Paul as a Christian refuted such folly (3:12-14). However, he knew how a person could consider himself blameless. There was a time in his life when he sincerely thought he had kept the laws of God. He was like the rich young ruler who said of the Commandments, " 'All these I have observed from my youth' " (Luke 18:21). By the standards of himself and his associates Paul had attained the highest level of righteousness before God.

Philippians 3:7 marks the radical change in Paul's outlook and life: "But whatever gain I had, I counted as loss for the sake of Christ" (3:7). Paul does not go into the familiar events of his Damascus Road encounter. He simply sums up the end result of his conversion.

Paul used the language of accounting. He came to see that the sum total of all his assets should actually have been listed in the loss column. "Paul uses the language of a man who reckons up his wealth and finds that by some error he has put to the credit side what had been his losses, and under this delusion has been hastening toward ruin."[7]

His heritage was a rich one, but he had been wrong to assume this made him better than others or placed him in special divine favor. Even worse was his blind pride in his legal righteousness. And worst of all was his assumption that he had been serving God by persecuting Christians.

In retrospect he saw the irony of it all. He had trusted all these things to make him right with God. Yet these were his worst sins because they stood between him and God, they set him against God's people, and they blinded him to God's will for his own life.

At this stage in his life he also probably understood why Jesus had such harsh things to say about the Pharisees. Jesus, for example, said, " 'Unless your righteousness exceeds that of the scribes and Pharisees, you will never enter the kingdom of heaven' " (Matt. 5:20). No statement would have been more shocking to Paul before his conversion. But now he understood that Pharisaic righteousness was based on a superficial view of the law and of sin. If the law can be reduced to external laws of behavior, legal righteousness is possible. But if the law probes human motivations, attitudes, values, and relationships, no one can claim perfection.

The key factor in Paul's conversion was his encounter with Christ. This is what caused him to count all his former gains as loss. From one point of view Paul gave up considerable assets to follow Christ. He gave up his status as a Pharisee, his reputation as a zealous leader in the movement, and his success as a keeper of the laws and traditions. In exchange he joined the small band of followers of

Jesus—people who were despised and persecuted. However, Paul did not see things from this point of view. Whatever he had given up should have been given up long before. Whatever difficulties he faced as a Christian were worth it all.

A good parallel to Philippians 3:7 is Jesus' parable of the pearl of great price (Matt. 13:45-46). The merchant sold all he had to gain the priceless pearl. Paul had found in Christ the pearl of great price.

"The Necklace" is a moving short story by the French writer Guy de Maupassant. A poor couple borrows a beautiful diamond necklace from a wealthy friend. The necklace is lost. The frantic couple buys from a jeweler an expensive necklace just like the borrowed one. They spend years paying off the debt, only to discover that the original necklace, which was lost, had been only an imitation.

Many people go through life under the delusion that the imitation is real. This delusion robs them of time, energy, opportunities, and often of life itself. Fortunate is the person who encounters the One whom to know is life indeed—abundant and eternal life. He has lost nothing and gained everything by exchanging the cheap imitation for the genuine priceless pearl.

A New Life (3:8-11)

In the early Christian centuries there were periods of violent persecution. A young officer witnessed the courage and hope of the Christian martyrs. Deeply impressed, he asked some Christians to tell him their secret, and they shared with him the good news of God's love in Jesus Christ. At the next hearing for people accused of being Christians, the young officer made known his new faith. The officers of the court asked: "Are you mad? Do you wish to throw away your life?" The new convert replied: "I am not mad. I was mad once but now I am in my right mind."[8]

Paul felt the same way as he viewed his old life from the perspective of his life in Christ. Like the prodigal son in Jesus' story, Paul had "come to himself." He saw things as they were for the first time. This new outlook turned life inside out for him.

Verses 7 and 8 are similar in many ways. Verse 8 expands and enlarges the thought from verse 7. The main difference is that Paul used the present tense for "count" in verse 8. Paul was writing from the perspective of years of Christian experience. He wanted his readers to know that the feeling expressed in verse 7 was not an impulsive mood connected only with the initial impetus of his conversion. What was true of his outlook at conversion was even more true after years of knowing and serving Christ.

Marvin Vincent paraphrases Paul's thought in verses 7-8 like this: "Since the hour of my conversion my estimate of the worthlessness of my legal righteousness and its profits has not changed. I continue to count them all but loss as compared with the surpassing worth of the knowledge of Christ Jesus my Lord."[9]

The last part of verse 8 introduces a new note that extends throughout the rest of the chapter: the tension between the present and the future. Do the words "that I may gain Christ" refer to what he had already gained in knowing Christ or to what he was yet to gain in knowing Christ? The same question can be asked about the words "that I may. . .be found in him" in verses 8-9 and "that I may know him" in verse 10.

Paul had both a present and a future reference. It was character- istic of Paul to speak of Christian experience as a present possession and as a future hope. What we have in Christ is already real and precious, but this reality holds in prospect a fulfillment even more wonderful than anything we have yet experienced. On the one hand, Paul already had gained Christ, was already found in him, and already knew him. On the other hand, gaining Christ, being found in him, and knowing him in the fullest sense were yet future.

This paradox holds true of nearly every Pauline concept. He spoke of *salvation* as past, present, and future (see comments on 2:12-13 and 3:20).

Righteousness is another key Pauline concept. Notice what he wrote in verse 9. To get the whole thought in context, read again also the last part of verse 8: "For his sake I have suffered the loss of all things, and count them as refuse, in order that I may gain Christ and be found in him, not having a righteousness of my own, based on law, but that which is through faith in Christ, the righteousness from God that depends on faith."

Paul's Roman and Galatian letters are the best commentaries on his concept of righteousness. First of all, Paul taught that when a sinner trusts Christ, he is justified or put right with God. This act of justifying the ungodly was deeply offensive to those who shared Paul's former presuppositions about their own righteousness based on keeping the law. Paul defended his new view of justification on several grounds. For one thing, legal righteousness is not real righteousness. Paul's experience, observation, and study of the Scriptures convinced him that no one can be righteous enough to justify himself before God (Rom. 2:1 to 3:20).

What then is the sinner's hope? On the Damascus Road this question forced itself on Paul with terrible fury. His whole life had been devoted to making himself acceptable to God. Then suddenly he discovered how completely wrong he had been about everything—God, Jesus, himself, the church, the law. He deserved only condemnation. He had persecuted none other than the Messiah himself.

Doubtlessly he waited for the wrath of God to fall on him as he groveled blindly in the dust. But the blow did not fall! Instead God dealt kindly with him. How could this be? How could God treat such a sinner with such mercy and forbearance? Somewhere along the way Paul realized that the only answer was the love of God. Grace was the basis on which God accepted him when he was so unacceptable. As Paul pondered the meaning of it all, he realized that this is what the death and resurrection of Jesus were all about. In offering forgiveness to sinners, God did not ignore sin; rather he bore the cost and pain that always accompanies genuine forgiveness (Rom. 3:21-31).

On the basis of his grace God justifies sinners or puts them in a new right relation with him. On that basis also God's Spirit works in believers to motivate and empower righteous living (Rom. 5-8). This new righteousness is very different from the legal righteousness Paul once had sought. Paul referred to that as "a righteousness of my own, based on law" (Phil. 3:9). His new righteousness was "the righteousness from God that depends on faith" (v. 9). True Christian righteousness is as much a work of God's grace as justification. The gracious God is at work by his Spirit to create right thoughts, actions, and relationships.

Yet this righteousness is a future hope as well as a present possession. "For through the Spirit by faith, we wait for the hope of righteousness" (Gal. 5:5). The truly righteous person is the one who feels the tension between what he is and what God wants him to be. Paul addressed himself further to this in Philippians 2:12-21 (see chapter 7). Paul had been put right with God; he was already pressing on in his life in Christ; and he had made his goal to be found in him with all the righteousness God intended to be his by grace through faith.

Knowledge is another of Paul's key concepts. When Paul spoke of such basic ideas as salvation, righteousness, or knowledge, he was not thinking of separate virtues in a list of commendable Christian qualities. Rather the apostle tended to pour the totality of Christian experience into each concept. That is, whenever he was using one of these key concepts he was thinking of the total sweep and scope of Christian experience. Each concept has a different shade of meaning; but each can encompass the past, present, and future aspects of Christian experience.

In verse 8 Paul wrote of "the surpassing worth of knowing Christ Jesus my Lord." This speaks to the personal dimension of a relationship with Christ. Frank Stagg writes: "Knowing Christ is more than knowing about him. . . . It is the personal acquaintance which is possible when person meets person in an atmosphere of love and trust, where there is acceptance and commitment."[10]

Paul had encountered Christ on the Damascus Road. He had come to know him. The longer and better he knew Christ, the more he wanted to know him. This is the spirit of the words "that I may know him" in verse 10.

When you become acquainted with a kind, delightful, and multifaceted person, you want that acquaintance to develop into a warm friendship. When it does, you cherish times spent with your friend. The better you know him the better you want to know him. If this is true of knowing a friend, how much more true of knowing Jesus Christ!

Paul was thinking not only of communion with Christ but also of increasing likeness to Christ. "That I may know him and the power of his resurrection, and may share his sufferings, becoming like him in his death, that if possible I may attain the resurrection from the dead" (3:10-11).

Resurrection is another key Pauline concept to set alongside salvation, righteousness, and knowledge. Paul used it to describe the past, present, and future of Christian experience. We were dead in trespasses and sins, but God made us alive and raised us up (Eph. 2:1,4). We were raised to walk in newness of life (Rom. 6:4; Col. 3:1). The Spirit of God that raised Jesus from the dead is the enabling power at work in believers (Eph. 1:19-20; Rom. 8:11). The future resurrection is the culmination of this resurrection life (Rom. 8:11; 1 Cor. 15).

Paul's point in Philippians 3:10-11 with regard to resurrection is this: He is striving to know more completely the power of the resurrected Christ in his life here and now. The future resurrection is his hope and goal. But he is not simply waiting for the resurrection, he is earnestly pressing on in the resurrection life.

Interpreters are puzzled by the words "if possible I may attain" in verse 11. Was Paul expressing some doubt about sharing in the future resurrection? Such uncertainty would be hard to explain in light of his many confident assertions about the resurrection (Phil. 3:20-21; 1 Cor. 15:51-57). The only uncertainty Paul seems to have expressed was related to the time of the resurrection and whether or not he would still be alive when Christ came (2 Cor. 5:1-10).

There apparently were people in the Philippian church who claimed perfection. One such group may have been a Gnostic-like group that denied a future bodily resurrection (Cf. 2 Tim. 2:17-18). Paul seems to have had such a group in mind in Philippians 3:12-21. Very likely, therefore, verse 11 should be seen in this setting. The

Gnostics claimed to have attained. They boasted of their present status by virtue of having already experienced the resurrection. By contrast, Paul insisted that experiencing the power of the resurrection does not lead to presumption and self-assertion. Rather it spurs one on toward the fulfillment of the resurrection life in the future resurrection of the body.

Compare 1 John 3:1-3: John rejoiced in the glorious status of being children of God and in the glorious hope of being like Christ at his coming. But he said that the mark of a child of God who shares that hope is that he is striving here and now to become more like Christ.

Philippians 3:10 speaks not only of knowing Christ's resurrection power but also of sharing Christ's sufferings and becoming like him in his death. The cross and resurrection were inseparable in Christ's mission. Neither alone constitutes the gospel. Likewise they are inseparable in Christian experience. The purpose of knowing Christ's resurrection power is to show forth the same kind of self-giving love that was central in his living and dying.

Christ's invitation to discipleship is an invitation to self-denial and crossbearing (Matt. 16:24; Luke 9:23). This is more than a matter of trying to follow Christ's example. Rather it is a way of life made possible by the indwelling presence of the Christ who died and was raised from the dead. This is the point of Paul's frequent references to being crucified with or dying with Christ (Gal. 2:20; 2 Cor. 5:14-15). Christians are enabled to die to self and sin by the resurrection power at work in us (Rom. 6:1-11).

Here is one of the closest ties between Philippians 3 and what Paul said earlier in the letter. The whole point in chapter 2 was Paul's appeal to share the mind of Christ, the way of humble, self-giving love that led Christ to the cross. Paul's commitment was to that way; his earnest prayer and continual goal was to give himself more completely to Christ and thus to have Christ's love and power work more freely in and through his life.

Clovis Chappell tells of a woman who said to him: " 'I used to say before I entered the Church, "If ever I become a Christian, I am going to be the right kind of Christian." But I am about like the rest. It has not really made much difference.' "[11]

There is a world of difference between her sad lament and Paul's vibrant testimony. How can we explain the difference? In some cases, the problem is that conversion was unreal or that, if genuine, it was left incomplete by failing to press on in commitment.

William Barclay addresses the problem. He points to the many gradations of how people try to relate to God. Many do so only on the most superficial level. Others profess faith but compartmentalize God, calling on him only in crises. Barclay gives this analysis of the basic difference between superficial religion and genuine commitment: "The one characteristic of all these attitudes to God is that in none of them is God the steadily dominant factor in life; in none of them does a man live in a permanent awareness of God; in none of them is a man permanently turned in the direction of God; in none of them is God the centre of life. In real conversion a man is turned around and left permanently facing God. For him the presence of the risen Christ is the very atmosphere of life. He is as much *in Christ*, in Paul's great phrase, as he is in the air which surrounds him and which gives him the breath of life."[12]

7

The Pilgrim View of Life

Philippians 3:12-21

"Instant" is one of the words that characterizes our age. The word is used, for example, to describe various foods and drinks that can be prepared instantly, usually only by adding boiling water.

Part of the frustration of our age is that the real needs and issues have no instant solutions. People wonder why the same technology that can develop instant foods cannot develop equally quick, simple solutions in other areas.

Some people always have seen religion as one of those "instant" solutions for the human dilemma. Indeed the way of Christ is sometimes presented as a simple answer to life's questions, a quick cure for life's ills, and a shortcut to life's goals. There is some truth in this presentation, but there is enough error for it to be false and deceptive. The Bible presents Christ as the answer, the cure, the way; but the Bible never uses the words *simple, quick, shortcut.*

On the one hand, the Bible clearly presents a personal relation with Christ as the decisive factor in life. There often is a radical difference between a person before and after meeting Christ. There is forgiveness of sins, a new relationship with God, the presence of God's Spirit, a new sense of purpose and direction, a new hope and assurance.

Yet, on the other hand, the Christian life is presented in terms of movement, growth, struggle. There are no simple answers to life's dilemmas. There are no quick formulas for instant maturity. There are no shortcuts from the beginning to the end of the Christian pilgrimage.

One of the biblical analogies for this reality is *pilgrimage.* The King James translation of Hebrews 11:13 refers to people of faith as "strangers and pilgrims." The Greek word means one who comes from a foreign country into a land and resides there beside the natives. Thus the word can properly be translated exile, refugee, or pilgrim. The context of Hebrews 11 favors "pilgrim." One dictionary meaning of pilgrim is a person who passes through life as if in exile from a heavenly homeland or in search of it or of some high goal. The people in Hebrews 11 were living on earth; but they were living by the values of the invisible, heavenly realm they sought.

Our use of the pilgrim analogy has been further shaped and enriched by John Bunyan's classic allegory *The Pilgrim's Progress.* The man Christian set out from the City of Destruction toward the yet unseen destination, the Celestial City. His conversion was crucial in the journey; but it occurred near the beginning of a long, arduous pilgrimage. His way was beset by all kinds of trials and temptations. He encountered all kinds of people—some were fellow pilgrims; many were not. The way was not short, quick, or easy; but Christian followed it because it was *the way.*

Some of his worst setbacks came when he was lured aside from the way to what appeared to be a pleasant shortcut to his goal. He strayed into By-path Meadow and ended up in Doubting Castle under the tyranny of Giant Despair. But Christian and his companion Hopeful eventually escaped using the key called Promise. Christian pressed on until finally he crossed the River of Death and arrived in the Celestial City.

In Philippians 3 Paul did not use the word *pilgrim* to describe himself, but his description of his Christian experience reflects the pilgrim view of life. His encounter with Christ was decisive; it turned life inside out (3:3-7). From that time his entire life was shaped by his commitment to become what Christ would have him to be (3:8-11). This was a goal that Paul had not yet attained but toward which he constantly was pressing on (3:12-14). Paul's definition of true perfection is seeking to narrow the gap between what he is and what Christ would have him become (3:15-16).

Those who claim to have already arrived morally and spiritually are usually those who are farthest from what they claim (3:17-19). True Christians recognize that they should live on earth as loyal citizens of the heavenly kingdom (3:20-21).

Pressing On the Upward Way (3:12-14)

Paul obviously did not believe in instant Christian maturity. Over the centuries there have been various groups who have claimed some sort of Christian perfection. Very likely there were those in Philippi who made such a claim. Paul made his own position clear when he wrote: "Not that I have already obtained this or am already perfect; but I press on to make it my own, because Christ Jesus has made me his own. Brethren, I do not consider that I have made it my own; but one thing I do, forgetting what lies behind and straining forward to what lies ahead, I press on toward the goal for the prize of the upward call of God in Christ Jesus" (3:12-14).

What is "this" in verse 12 that Paul had not yet obtained? The apostle was referring to verses 8-11, where he had described his goal in terms of the full knowledge of Christ and his righteousness and of fully sharing in Christ's death and resurrection. Paul presented each of these as a past reality, a present experience, and a future hope (see comments in preceding chapter).

Verse 12 spells out what is implicit in verses 8-11. Paul knew Christ; he was striving to know him better; but he had not arrived at a perfect knowledge. Paul had been put right with God; he was growing in righteousness; but perfect righteousness remained a hope, not an attainment. Paul had passed from death to life through the crucified, risen Lord; he was seeking to let Christ show his love and resurrection power in him; but the final resurrection was still future.

Thus Paul had not attained these things; he was not already perfect. However, he was pressing on. The Greek word translated "press on" is the same word used in verse 6 to describe Saul's persecution of the church. It means to pursue something. The non-Christian Saul had zealously *pursued* the church as a persecutor; the

Christian Paul zealously *pursued* what Christ wanted him to be. The same word is used again in verse 14, when Paul developed the analogy of an athlete bending every effort toward crossing the finish line.

Paul wrote, "I press on to make it my own, because Christ Jesus has made me his own." Thus he clearly rooted his present pressing on and his future hope in his past encounter with Christ. Initially Christ laid hold on Paul for a purpose. From that time on Paul was continually pressing on toward that purpose.

Verse 13 gives added insight into what Paul meant by "pressing on." The words "one thing I do" indicate the concentration of Paul's energies on this endeavor. The endeavor itself involved two aspects: "forgetting what lies behind and straining forward to what lies ahead."

What was it Paul sought to forget? It may have been the shame of the memory of his old life prior to meeting Christ. No one who is haunted by the guilt of past sins can move forward vigorously for Christ. However, this probably was not what he had in mind. He likely was thinking of past successes and accomplishments, not past failures and sins.

Paul had made progress in the Christian life. He had had some deep meaningful spiritual experiences. He had been used by God to accomplish some real breakthroughs for the gospel. In other words, if Paul had been looking for evidences of moral and spiritual attainments, he could have found them. But he deliberately forgot those things. He resisted the temptation to let pride in past accomplishments lead to the snare of complacency and self-satisfaction.

Paul's old life had been built on pride in supposed moral and spiritual attainments. He now recognized how wrong that had been—that old confidence in the flesh (3:3-7). He was determined that he would not make the same mistake as a Christian.

There were times in his ministry when Paul mentioned some of his attainments. For example, in dealing with his critics in Corinth, Paul found himself confronted with people who boasted of their own moral and spiritual attainments. They used these as evidence of their alleged susperiority to Paul, who considered such boasting foolish and unchristian (2 Cor. 10). But to refute their claims, he sometimes challenged them with a list of his own accomplishments (2 Cor. 11, especially vv. 24-29). Paul apologized for such "boasting." He would prefer to boast only of the Lord (2 Cor. 10:17) and of his own weakness (2 Cor. 11:30).

Second Corinthians 10—12 is good background for Philippians 3:13—in fact, for many other things in chapter 3. Paul had not "forgotten" the past in the sense of erasing things from his memory. He recalled past accomplishments and listed them in 2 Corinthians. However, Paul had "forgotten" those things in the sense of ever letting them nurture pride or complacency.

In his pilgrimage Paul was not only forgetting past accomplishments but also "straining forward to what lies ahead." At this point Paul seems to have been thinking of an athlete in a race. This clearly was in his mind in verse 14. Marvin Vincent sees this picture of the runner in the last part of verse 13: "The body of the racer is bent forward, his hand is outstretched toward the goal, and his eye is fastened upon it."[1]

Paul and other biblical writers used athletic analogies from time to time (1 Cor. 9:24-27; Phil. 1:27; 2 Tim. 2:5; 4:7-8). One of the most vivid comparisons of the Christian life to a race is in Hebrews 12:1. After listing the past heroes of faith who persevered in their pilgrimages, the writer said, "Therefore, since we are surrounded by so great a cloud of witnesses, let us also lay aside every weight, and sin which clings so closely, and let us run with perseverance the race that is set before us."

In what ways is the Christian life like a race? For one thing, it requires training and rigid self-discipline. Second, it calls for keeping at it. Perseverance is the explicit point in Hebrews 12:1. The Christian life is not like the hundred-yard dash but the long-distance run, the marathon, the cross-country run.

At this point, the analogies of race and pilgrimage converge. Both require perseverance. Neither can be run quickly, with one burst of energy. There are no shortcuts, no instant victories. The secret is perseverance.

A third similarity is earnest effort and concentration. This is the emphasis in Philippians 3:14. The "goal" that the runner bears down on is "the mark on the race track at the finish line to which the athlete directs his eye."[2]

The prize is "the upward call of God in Christ Jesus." This upward calling was not Paul's unique call to be an apostle but the call that all Christians hear and heed. At this point the analogy of a race breaks down. In most races there can be only one winner. In this race there are many winners. Christians "share in a heavenly calling" (Heb. 3:1). God's purpose and our hope are bound up in God's calling (Eph. 1:18; 4:4). Philippians 3:8-11 describes some of the content of that upward calling. God calls us to fullness of life in Christ.

This becomes the Christian's hope, but it is not his hope in the sense that he can only wait patiently to receive it. True hope also calls forth persistent and earnest effort on our part. Patient waiting is one side of hope. It reminds us that the fulfillment of hope, like every other aspect of the Christian life, is a gift of God's grace not a human attainment. But the other side of hope is that it becomes the goal toward which we continue to strive throughout our pilgrimage.

True Perfection (3:15-16)

When a person is accepted to become a minister in the Methodist Church, he is asked a question that John Wesley began asking two hundred years ago: "Are you going on to perfection?" Gerald Kennedy tells how when a young man objected to the question, an older man asked him: "All right, son. What are you going on to?"[3]

Paul followed up on his words of verses 12-14 by writing, "Let those of us who are mature be thus minded; and if in anything you are otherwise minded, God will reveal that also to you. Only let us hold true to what we have attained" (3:15-16).

The word translated "mature" in verse 15 is a cognate of the word translated "perfect" in verse 12. At times the meaning of the word is perfect in the absolute sense. For example, Jesus said: " 'You, therefore, must be perfect, as your heavenly Father is perfect' " (Matt. 5:48). At other times "mature" in the sense of full-grown is a better translation. The writer of Hebrews, for example, was speaking of those who ought to have moved beyond a diet of milk to solid food: "For every one who lives on milk is unskilled in the word of righteousness, for he is a child. But, solid food is for the mature" (Heb. 5:13-14).

There are at least two possible translations and interpretations of Philippians 3:15. According to one view, when Paul used "perfect," he had in mind a group in the Philippian church who claimed to be perfect. They may have been Judaizers (3:2-3) who boasted of their circumcision as a badge of full Christian attainment. They may have been persons with Gnostic tendencies, who boasted of perfect moral and spiritual attainments. There may have been some of both.

If so, Paul was being ironic in verse 15. He was challenging those who boasted of being "perfect" to realize what is true perfection. True perfection, according to Paul, is to recognize our imperfection but continually to seek to narrow the gap between what we are and what we should be.

According to the other interpretation, Paul was not being ironic. He was not thinking of a special group of "perfectionists" when he used "mature" in verse 15. Rather he was appealing to all the Philippians to recognize that Christian maturity does not involve a claim to perfection but does involve pressing on toward perfection.

Frank Stagg calls attention to the paradox involved in comparing verse 15 with verse 12: "Paradoxically, one can be perfect (mature) only if he disclaims perfection as an attainment and affirms it as a goal."[4]

Complacency is the deadly enemy of Christian pilgrims. Nothing is so effective in thwarting further progress toward Christian maturity. In some cases, the complacency is based on a pride that blinds people into believing that they already have attained moral and spiritual excellence.

A person may or may not actually claim to be perfect; but if he considers himself as good or religious as he needs to be, the end result is the same. He cuts the tension between what he is and what God wants him to be. He settles into a complacent rut.

Another paradox is at work here. The closer a person is to Christ the more aware he is of the gap that separates him from perfection. On the other hand, the farther one is from Christ the less likely he is to be aware of the moral and spiritual dearth of his life. This explains how a person like Paul could be so deeply in earnest about pressing on toward perfection; whereas many a nominal Christian gives little or no attention to growth in grace. The latter group has hardly begun the Christian pilgrimage before settling down safely and securely at some point far from the distant goal.

What did Paul mean in the last part of verse 15? Some interpreters believe Paul was expressing a measure of tolerance for a point of view different from his own. That is, "believe the truth as you see it, and God will lead you eventually to the larger truth."[5] However, the emphasis is probably on the words "God will reveal that also to you." That is, God will reveal the real truth, which Paul had stated, to anyone who is open to God's revelation. Ralph Martin believes that Paul was addressing a perfectionist group or groups in verse 15. If so, in effect Paul said, "If—as you claim—so much has been revealed to you, then no doubt God will reveal *that* to you also."[6]

Verse 16 is another verse that is hard to translate and to interpret. A literal translation is, "Only as far as we have attained by the same let us walk." Paul was following up on his statement in the preceding verse in which he called on them to share his understanding of perfection. To those who did not share his view, Paul said that he expected God to reveal it to them. His follow-up in verse 16 seems to be a call to be faithful to that way in which they had been instructed. Whatever new insight or revelation they received would be consistent with what Paul had shown them by word and deed. In fact, one condition on which they might expect new light was to act according to the light they already had received.

Confusing Sensuality with Spirituality (3:17-19)

To some modern readers Paul's words in verse 17 may seem to deny the whole theme of Philippians. Who but an egotist would say, "Brethren, join in imitating me"?

This accusation overlooks several important facts. For one thing, the moral confusion in the Greco-Roman world was great. How were the converts from paganism to learn about Christian living? Words were not enough. They needed examples, models of what a Christian says and does. The first Christian missionaries in any such environment inevitably become the examples to which new converts look. Paul did not back off from this duty. He tried to set a good example of Christian living. He knew the new converts needed this.

Second, keep the context in mind. Paul had just stated very clearly that he was not perfect. Thus he did not set himself forth as a perfect example. In fact, he had just told them that the only worthy example of a Christian is the person who admits he is not perfect but is nonetheless pressing on.

Third, notice that Paul called on them to imitate not only him but also others who had followed Paul's example and teachings. He wrote, "Mark those who so live as you have an example in us." Earlier he had referred to Timothy and Epaphroditus as two such persons (2:19-30).

After reading 3:18-19, it becomes more obvious why Paul wrote what he did in verse 17: "For many, of whom I have often told you and now tell you even with tears, live as enemies of the cross of Christ. Their end is destruction, their god is the belly, and they glory in their shame, with minds set on earthly things."

Who were these people? Paul obviously felt very strongly about them. He issued a strongly-worded warning about them.

One of the problems in understanding Philippians is identifying the persons referred to in 1:15-17; 3:2; and 3:18-19. In each case Paul mentioned some people with whom he disagreed. Were these the same people, or were they from different groups? The evidence is not strong enough to be dogmatic; however they seem to have been from different groups. The people in 1:15-17 were preaching Christ, but they were not doing so for the right reasons. Thus their motives were wrong, not their basic message. The people in 3:2 seem to have been Jewish legalists, probably Judaizers, professing faith in Jesus as Messiah but demanding circumcision and keeping the law. The group in 3:18-19 seems to have been yet a third group. Parts of their description could have fit the Judaizers, but it is unlikely that one group could have combined all the characteristics of the Judaizers with what Paul said in 3:18-19.

More than likely, the group described in 3:18-19 were libertines or antinomians, probably with Gnostic presuppositions (cf. comments on 1:15-17; 3:2). Elsewhere in Paul's letters, Paul reflects a running battle with two groups—legalists and libertines. He wrote to the Galatian churches to warn them against becoming enslaved by legalism (Gal. 5:1), but he also warned against interpreting freedom selfishly and irresponsibly (Gal. 5:13). Christians are free from the law as a means of attaining or maintaining a right relation with God. However, this freedom is under the responsible compulsion of *agape* and of the Spirit (Gal. 5:13-26).

Paul's Roman letter also reflects a position that refutes legalism without embracing libertinism. Some of the libertines apparently were claiming that Paul's teachings led ultimately to their position. In other words, since we are sinners saved by grace, why not continue in sin that grace can abound (Rom. 6:1)? And since we are no longer under law but grace, why not ignore the law's moral demands (Rom. 6:15)? Romans 6—8 is Paul's refutation of such distortions of the gospel of grace.

Many if not all of these libertine groups were Gnostic in outlook. That is, they claimed special wisdom and spiritual insight, which put them in a unique category of the spiritually elite. Frank Stagg gives this summary of their views: "Some in the early church thought of themselves as 'spiritual,' having a special knowledge of God, and claimed to be above sin. They held that they were essentially soul or 'spirit' and that the body was only a temporary house, of no enduring value. Those holding such a dualism, spirit as good and matter as evil or worthless, became either ascetic or libertine. The ascetics called the body evil and tried to suppress it. The libertines called it insignificant, and claimed freedom to do as they pleased with it."[7]

The Gnostic tendencies in Colossae seem to have resulted in ascetic tendencies (Col. 2:18-23). By contrast, Gnostic tendencies in the Corinthian church created a dangerous libertinism.[8] The Corinthians argued that since sex is a purely physical function, sexual practices have nothing to do with morals, which have to do only with spiritual things (1 Cor. 6:12-13).

Paul's words in Philippians 3:18-19 seem to bear out the thesis that this group was not confined to Philippi. Frank Stagg notes that they "are identified as to destiny and character but not otherwise. It is not possible to identify their place of residence, whether in Philippi or elsewhere. Since they are *many* and Paul has *often* warned against them, possibly they are not limited to any one place."[9] In other words, Paul's words are consistent with the view that Gnostic libertines were problems in more than one place. We cannot tell how many were in Philippi or how strong was their influence there. However, the inclusion of this warning shows that the threat was real enough for Paul to repeat an earlier warning against such libertines.

They "live as enemies of the cross of Christ." Some Gnostics denied basic Christian doctrines—the creation, incarnation, atonement, and resurrection. In this sense they were enemies of the cross. However, in Philippians 3:18 Paul probably was thinking more about their life-style than their doctrine. Their way of life was completely contradictory to the way of the cross. The way of the cross as defined in Philippians 2:1-11 is the way of humble, self-giving love that draws Christians together in a common life and purpose. The libertine Gnostics fostered proud self-assertion and self-indulgence, both of which led also to disruptive dissension.

Their sensuality and moral self-indulgence is depicted by Paul's words "Their god is the belly." This graphic description implies such sins as fornication, drunkenness, gluttony.

"They glory in their shame." The libertines not only condoned and practiced immoral acts, they actually gloried in their freedom to do such things. First Corinthians 5:1-2 indicates that they not only condoned a shameful case of incest; they were proud and arrogant about it. Thus, when Paul wrote "They glory in their shame," he probably meant that "they boast of conduct that ought to be regarded as shameful."[10]

Strangely enough, the libertines, in spite of their evil lives, were proud and complacent. Paul's words about perfection in verses 12-16 may have been addressed at least partially to them.

Ralph Martin sees the claim to perfection as one thing in common between the legalists of 3:2 and the libertines of 3:18-19. If so, this helps explain the structure of chapter 3. Paul warned of legalists (3:2-3). Then he told of his own experience (3:4-11), and specifically denied having attained perfection (3:12-16). Then he warned of libertines (3:17-19). The verses about perfection tie the two warnings together. Both legalists and libertines were proud and complacent, some even to the point of claiming perfection.

How could the evil, sensual libertines claim perfection? They did so by claiming that their souls were saved and enlightened; therefore, what they did with their bodies did not matter.

Their "minds" were "set on earthly things." They had cut the tension between present experience and future hope. Everything focused on here and now. They were like those who denied the future resurrection because they claimed they had already experienced the resurrection (2 Tim. 2:18). Thus, they were subject to no upward heavenly calling. They were on no pilgrimage, because they believed that they already had arrived. This absence of eschatological hope and moral tension stands in sharp contrast to Paul's view, to which he turned again in verses 20-21.

Before turning to those verses, however, let us ask about the relevance of verses 18-19. In every generation Christianity must do battle with the two equally false extremes of legalism and libertinism. Each keeps taking new forms and calling itself by new names, but each stands in contradiction to the heart of the Christian gospel of grace.

Legalism is the more subtle danger and is most often found clothed in religious terminology and advocated by people within the church. However, many decent godless people outside the church also live by a form of legalism. They have reduced the biblical message to commonplace moral expectations. They often feel no need for God, Christ, salvation, or the church. Their religion is the Golden Rule or the Sermon on the Mount or the Ten Commandments, which they usually water down to fit the life-style of decent, respectable people like themselves.

Libertinism is the more powerful force at work today. Under the assault of a combination of philosophies and social trends, traditional morality has taken a beating. Increasing numbers of people have no deep moral convictions. Moral absolutes are things of the past; moral relativism is the "in" thing. The end result is often a kind of self-indulgence similar to that of the Gnostic libertines. Most of the descriptions in verses 18-19 could just as appropriately have been written by some modern Paul in the twentieth century.

Citizens of a Heavenly Kingdom (3:20-21)

Contrasting himself to those who set their minds on earthly things, Paul wrote: "But our commonwealth is in heaven, and from it we await a Savior, the Lord Jesus Christ, who will change our lowly body to be like his glorious body, by the power which enables him even to subject all things to himself" (3:20-21).

The word translated "commonwealth" can mean "way of life," but the basic meaning is "citizenship." A verb form of the word is found in Philippians 1:27. The people of Philippi had a special status. Philippi was a colony of Rome. This was quite an honor to be conferred on a city. It meant that they were citizens of Rome with all the privileges and responsibilities of Romans (see Acts 16:21). Although the city of Philippi was hundreds of miles from Rome, the people considered themselves a loyal outpost of the distant capital city. They were to keep its laws and reflect its ways.

Paul may have been consciously building on this situation in Philippi when he reminded the Christians there that their real citizenship is in heaven. (See comments on Phil. 1:27.) There may even have been an intended analogy to the occasional visits of the emperor to Philippi when Paul spoke of Christians awaiting the coming of the Savior. The word *Savior* was used of emperors, even one like Nero. Paul reminded believers of the true Savior, the Lord Jesus Christ.

We cannot be sure what special significance the Philippian Christians saw in Paul's description in verse 20. We do know that the basic idea of being earthly pilgrims seeking a heavenly city was widely held among early Christians. Paul used it in more than one of his letters (Gal. 4:26; Eph. 2:19). Peter addressed his readers as "aliens and exiles" (1 Pet. 2:11). The writer of Hebrews expounded on it in the famous faith chapter (Heb. 11:13,16).

Hebrews 11 is a good parallel passage to be read with Philippians 3:20. The writer saw people like Abraham as strangers and pilgrims on earth. Abraham journeyed to and resided in a land that was not his own, but that God had promised to him and his descendants. The writer saw this as reflecting the true situation of all people of faith. We are pilgrims on earth on our way to a homeland; but this homeland is not any earthly land or country. Rather, it is "a better country, that is, a heavenly one" (Heb. 11:16).

This is the basic biblical idea behind Bunyan's allegory. Christian was on a journey from the City of Destruction to the Celestial City. That was his destination and true home. He was a stranger and pilgrim in the places through which he passed on his journey. The challenge was to remain true to the standards of his true homeland rather than being shaped by the values of the lands through which he passed.

Without a doubt Paul intended his readers to see their heavenly citizenship as a challenge to how they lived. The context of Philippians 3 makes this clear. Paul's hope was eschatological, future, beyond him. This kept taut the tension between what he was and what Christ would have him to be. Heaven was not "pie-in-the-sky, by-and-by"; it was his hope and thus the goal of his earthly pilgrimage. His values were the values of heaven, not earth.

Part of the problem with Paul's opponents was that they had cut loose from this future hope and goal. Thus they settled for what they were, and they accepted the values of where they were. The people described in verses 18-19 were not being constantly drawn forward in hope and conduct by a vision of a heavenly city governed by divine will. Rather they saw only the here and now; they set their minds on earthly things.

Leonard Griffith tells of a minister who made this statement at a funeral service: "My friends, we are living for two worlds." Later he was challenged by a successful man of the world who said: "We are living for one world and one world only. We do not know of any other world than this one." The minister asked: "If you did believe in another world, would it make any difference to you?" The man replied: "Of course it would. If I had the slightest suspicion we are really living for any other world than this, I should change every major business policy before night."[11]

Philippians 3:20-21 describes the consummation toward which Paul's hope was directed. It involved the coming of the Lord Jesus Christ, whom Paul here referred to as Savior. In connection with this coming, Paul hoped for the transformation of the body and the subjection of all things to Christ.

F. W. Beare observes: "Paul speaks of our expectation of the future, not in terms of our 'going to heaven,' but in terms of Christ coming *from heaven*."[12] The primary focus of biblical hope is directed toward the final consummation of God's redemptive work, not to the survival of the individual beyond death. This is one of the basic differences between the biblical hope of resurrection and the philosophical hope of immortality of the soul. The latter is most concerned about whether or not the individual will survive death. The former is most concerned with God's purpose which transcends death and includes all his people.

Philippians 1:21-23 reflects Paul's hope that when death came, he would go to be with Christ. Philippians 3:20-21 reflects his more basic hope for the consummation of God's purpose, which includes both the dead in Christ and those still alive when Christ comes (see comments on Phil. 1:21-23).

Christ will come as "Savior." The New Testament concept of salvation is much richer than what is often preached and taught as salvation. It is broader in scope, including not only deliverance from sin but also from all that threatens and limits earthly life. The word "salvation" in Greek means deliverance, wholeness, health.

When Paul wrote of salvation, he sometimes spoke in future terms (Rom. 5:9-10; 13:11). He also could speak of salvation as something already accomplished (Eph. 2:8; Titus 3:5) and even as something going on in present experience (Phil. 2:12). Like other Pauline descriptions of God's work in us, he spoke of salvation as a past event, a present experience, and a future hope. Paul was not looking for Jesus Christ to come again as Savior in the way he did in his incarnate work. Rather the apostle awaited the one whom he had already come to know as Savior, but the one who would come to complete what salvation had already begun in him and others (Phil. 1:6).

This consummation of salvation includes the transformation of our earthly body into a glorified body like Christ's. The King James translation "vile body" is unfortunate. This has contributed to the false notion that the body is evil or worthless. Literally Paul wrote "the body of our humiliation." Our bodies are not evil or worthless; however they are subject to the aging process and finally to death; they are subject to all manner of earthly injuries and diseases; and they are marred by sins—ours and the world's in which we live. The transformed and glorified body of Christian hope will be a body fit for the conditions of heaven. Paul's longest commentary on this is First Corinthians 15:20-57. Paul by no means answers all our questions about this new mode of existence, but he does insist that the glorified body is a body, not a disembodied soul. It is not the resuscitation of our flesh-and-blood bodies; but it is the continuing life of the human personality in an appropriate body for the new realm of life from which sickness, sin, and death are absent.

The consummation of salvation, like its beginning and its continuing, is a work of God's grace. Paul was always earnestly pressing on toward that hoped-for goal; but he saw no contradiction between God's grace and his best efforts. It was by grace that he was a Christian. Any progress in the Christian way was by God's grace at work in and through him. And when he experienced the full salvation and transformation at Christ's coming, that too would be by God's grace.

Thus Christian hope calls forth both diligence and patience. In one sense we work and pray for the coming kingdom; in another sense we await what only God can do. We make our best efforts with God's help, but we leave the rest to God.

William Barclay tells this story to illustrate this paradox: "There is a story about a boy who was trying to make a boat out of a piece of wood. He hacked away at it but could not get it to come right. Tired out and discouraged he went to bed, leaving the unfinished boat on a chair beside his bed. When he was sleeping his father came and saw it; and his father took the tools and the chisel and the wood and shaped it into a perfect boat, and when the boy woke in the morning the thing that beat him had been done."[13]

8

The Secret of Contentment

Philippians 4:1-23

In the early 1930's a scholarly man in Australia took a careful look at the world situation. He had enough foresight to predict another world war. He even realized that it would reach into the Pacific. The man was determined to escape such a catastrophe if he could. He began, therefore, a systematic search of his maps. He was seeking some remote spot to which he might retire in peace. Finally the scholar located just the spot. It was an almost unknown island far from the well-traveled paths of the sea. So in 1939 he went ashore on Guadalcanal.

This incident points up humanity's persistent, yet futile search for peace and contentment. This is a universal quest, but it is seldom a satisfying one. These qualities seem to elude the seeker like a mirage in the desert. And the very search often leads us farther and farther into the desert.

Philippians 4 is a classic biblical statement on the secret of contentment. No striking new themes are introduced in these final words of Paul to the Philippians. However, the last chapter in the letter is not just a recapitulation of earlier themes. As in earlier chapters, there is an emphasis on the words "joy" (4:1) and "rejoice" (4:4,10). Yet there is a new emphasis on the word "peace." Paul wrote of the "peace of God" (4:7) and of the "God of peace" (4:9).

Paul had mentioned earlier in the letter his gratitude for the Philippians' generous gift to him, but now he dealt with this in more detail. His words in verses 10-20 constitute one of the finest statements ever made of the twin graces of gratitude and contentment.

Blessed Are the Peacemakers (4:1-5)

Several of Paul's letters conclude with an exhortation to put into practice the concepts presented in the heart of the letter. The word "therefore" is prominent in such exhortations. (See, for example, Rom. 12:1; Gal. 5:1; Col. 3:5; Eph. 4:1). Philippians 4:1 is such a verse: "Therefore, my brethren, whom I love and long for, my joy and crown, stand firm thus in the Lord, my beloved."

This verse draws together a variety of expressions that show Paul's close relation with and high regard for the Philippians. In this sense it is reminiscent of 1:3-8, where Paul had stated his feelings for these partners in the gospel. Both passages stress that they were loved and longed for by Paul. He called them "my brethren . . . my joy and crown . . . my beloved."

Because Paul loved these people, who were his pride and joy, he continued to address them as a loving father would. He was bursting with pride, yet he also was concerned about their shortcomings. Thus he repeated the exhortation with which he earlier had dealt most explicitly with their need for oneness of Spirit: the word "stand firm" in 1:27 introduced 1:27 to 2:11, where Paul had stressed the need for oneness in Christ based on unselfish commitment. He wrote "stand firm *in one spirit*" in 1:27; he wrote "stand firm *in the Lord* in 4:1. The meaning is essentially the same in both verses. Oneness of Spirit is one thing involved in being "in the Lord."

Life in Christ is a key theme in all Paul's letters. We encountered it at the very beginning of Philippians (see comments on 1:1). This terminology of being *in the Lord* (or *in Christ Jesus* or *in him*) occurs eight times in chapter 4 (vv. 1,2,4,7,10,13,19,21).

Earlier Paul had hinted at problems of disunity in the church. Here he dealt directly with one such incident. Paul addressed two women in the church by name, Euodia and Syntyche; he urged them "to agree in the Lord" (4:2). When Paul first preached the gospel in Philippi, he preached to a group of women on a riverbank (Acts 16:13). Perhaps these two women were from that group. At any rate Paul says that these two had "labored side by side" with him in the gospel together with others in Philippi (4:3).

We do not have any clue as to what caused the falling out of these two prominent members of the church. The occasion for the falling out may have been related to the general spirit of disunity in the church; it may even have been a key factor in the church's problem. Paul obviously considered the situation serious enough to address the two personally in a letter to the entire church: "I entreat Euodia and I entreat Syntyche to agree in the Lord" (4:2). The repetition of "I entreat" makes the exhortation even more personal. Paul personally appealed to each woman to agree *in the Lord.*

The words translated "agree" literally mean to be thinking the same thing. The best commentary on this is 2:1-11. There Paul spelled out what it means to have the same mind in the Lord. To paraphrase 2:3-4 as it would apply to a rift between two persons: Do nothing from selfishness or conceit, but in humility count the other person better than yourself. Let each of you look not only to his (or her) own interests but also to the interests of the other person.

In verse 3 Paul addressed directly some other person in the Philippian church: "And I ask you also, true yokefellow, help these women, for they have labored side by side with me in the gospel together with Clement and the rest of my fellow workers, whose names are in the book of life." There has been much speculation about the identity of this "true yokefellow." Some have speculated that this was Paul's wife, and some have even speculated that Lydia was his wife. This is most unlikely in light of what Paul wrote in 1 Corinthians 7 about not being married. Lightfoot suggests that Epaphroditus was the "true yokefellow," but would Paul have addressed in this way the bearer of the letter? Others have suggested Timothy, but would Paul have addressed in this way someone still with him? Some commentators believe that the word translated "true yokefellow" was a proper noun, and that Paul thus addressed someone whose name was Syzygus. However, no one has found any other record of this word as a proper name.

Whoever the "true yokefellow" was, Paul gave him an important task: "help these women." The word translated "help" literally means to "take hold with." In other words, this person was to work with Euodia and Syntyche in reconciling their differences.

One of Jesus' Beatitudes is "Blessed are the peacemakers, for they shall be called the sons of God" (Matt. 5:9). The ministry of being a peacemaker is a hazardous venture. Peacemakers are often misunderstood and maligned. They often get caught in the crossfire in the no-man's-land of hostility between the warring partners. In other words, only two kinds of people ever venture into this ministry—naive people who don't know what they are getting into or concerned people who care enough to take the risks. Of the latter category, Jesus said they were "blessed" and that they would be called "the sons of God."

Paul mentions by name only one other person, Clement. However, he shows he held all of his fellow workers in Philippi in high regard. Although Paul did not pause to list all their names in his letter, he reminded them that their names were listed where it really counts, in the book of life.

Verse 4 is another summary verse that repeats a recurring theme in the letter: "Rejoice in the Lord always; again I will say, Rejoice." He followed this with another exhortation to practice what is needed for Christians to rejoice together in the Lord: "Let all men know your forbearance. The Lord is at hand" (4:5).

The word translated "forbearance" has the idea of thoughtfulness or consideration. It is the opposite of a rigid stand based on one's rights. In other words, it is a key quality in resolving differences of opinion, in reconciling persons with differences, and in maintaining on a high level any kind of personal relationships. Such forbearance is an essential part of Christian love.

The word *forbearance* applies to the relationships of Christians not only with one another but also with outsiders. The Philippian Christians were in an environment that was often hostile. They needed to be able to turn the other cheek (Matt. 5:38-47), to give back good for evil (Rom. 12:14-21), in other words to be gracious and forbearing.

The words "The Lord is at hand" reflect the early Christians' sense of the imminence of the Lord's coming. They took seriously the sayings of Jesus about watchfulness and preparedness. Their hope did not cause them to await passively the consummation; rather it exerted an ethical tension that affected their attitudes and actions.

The saying here may be connected with what precedes; that is, it motivates forbearance. Or it may be connected with what follows; that is, it motivates prayerful trust and gratitude. Or it may have a bearing both on what precedes and also on what follows. In the latter case, the connection may be like this: "Be forbearing; the Lord is at hand who will right all wrongs and give to each his due. Be not anxious. The Lord is at hand. Why be concerned about what is so soon to pass away? The Lord's coming will deliver you from all earthly care."[1]

Withdrawing from the world or from people is obviously not the secret of contentment. Peace as defined in the Bible is not achieved by arranging circumstances that are free from the inevitable dynamics and problems of human relationships. True peace, contentment, joy, blessedness can be known only by one who takes the risks inherent in Christian love and concern.

Anxiety and Prayer (4:6-7)

Verses 6-7 state another principle in the Bible's secret of contentment: "Have no anxiety about anything, but in everything by prayer and supplication with thanksgiving let your requests be made known to God. And the peace of God, which passes all understanding, will keep your hearts and your minds in Christ Jesus."

F. B. Meyer gives a clear outline of verse 6:[2]

1. Be anxious for nothing.
2. Be prayerful about everything.
3. Be thankful for anything.

The first of these points is reminiscent of the words of Jesus in the Sermon on the Mount. The recurring theme in Matthew 6:25-34 is "Do not be anxious." This admonition was relevant for the Philippians. They lived in a hostile pagan world. Their church was beset by problems within and without. In addition, most of them lived in economic circumstances where survival was a goal (see 2 Cor. 8:1-2).

The admonition is equally relevant for our troubled and anxious generation. We stand in much the same position as did Robinson Crusoe shortly after he arrived on his island. The lonely man built a dwelling, raised a stockade, planted a garden, and primed his gun. His knowledge of the island did not extend much beyond his small beachhead. He did not know but that at any moment wild beasts or heathen cannibals might emerge from the dark jungle. We also stand peering anxiously into the darkness around us and ahead of us, not knowing quite what to expect.

It may be of some comfort to remember that every age has had its own tension and anxiety. It may help also to recognize that many of our fears have no basis in fact. But any real release from anxiety must grow out of more fertile soil than this. Paul could shun anxiety not because he had no real problems but because of his spirit of grateful prayer. He could say "Be anxious for nothing" because he could also say "Be prayerful about everything" and "Be thankful for anything."

When the Assyrians were threatening the gates of Jerusalem, they sent an outrageous letter to King Hezekiah. The Old Testament writer says that the good king took the letter into the Temple and spread it before the Lord (2 Kings 19:14). Prayer is not often the only thing one can do in a bad situation, but it is always the first thing one should do.

Real prayer of course is made in a spirit of thanksgiving. Elsewhere Paul said, "In every thing give thanks" (1 Thess. 5:18, KJV). He did not say *for*, but *in*. "Give thanks in all circumstances." A Christian is not grateful *for* the painful experiences of life, but by God's grace a person can be grateful *in* dark times. This kind of joyful gratitude even in difficult times is one of Paul's themes. On his first visit to Philippi Paul had sung hymns after being cruelly and unjustly beaten and imprisoned (Acts 16:25). His entire Philippian letter reflects a spirit of joyful gratitude, even though he was a prisoner (see comments on 1:18-19). The secret of this gratitude is that a Christian has found the supreme blessing in fellowship with the Lord.

Paul says that this realization is the key to the incredible peace of God. This peace, he says, will keep or guard the heart and life of the believer as he journeys through life. This is the reason the Australian who ended up on Guadalcanal failed in his quest for peace. He thought that peace is the result of the skillful arrangement of outward circumstances so as to avoid trouble. He was apparently unaware that real peace is the result of the presence of God with a man as he passes over a sea of troubles.

The peace of God in verse 7 is the peace that God possesses and bestows. It is grounded in God's presence and promise. Such peace "passes all understanding," or it may mean "surpasses every thought." If the latter translation is correct, the idea is that this peace goes beyond anything the human mind can devise to try to insure contentment or tranquility. If the former translation is correct, the idea is that this peace works in a way that is beyond our ability to understand or explain.

Compare Paul's great prayer in Ephesians 3:14-21, which he concluded by committing his prayers "to him who by the power at work within us is able to do far more abundantly than all that we ask or think."

Allen Gardiner was a missionary to Patagonia. His ministry was one of those seemingly wasted efforts on the part of a courageous missionary pioneer. After all his privations and sacrifices he died on a desolate beach. When his body was found, his diary lay by his outstretched hand. His last entry in a shaky, half-legible scrawl contained these amazing words: "I am overwhelmed with a sense of the goodness of God."[3]

This is indeed an example of the "peace that passes understanding." Who can understand or explain this on human presuppositions? A modern Festus might conclude that his great sufferings had caused him to be deprived of his senses. It seems incredible that a man who had lost everything could say such a thing if he were in his right mind. But did not Jesus say, "Whoever would save his life will lose it, and whoever loses his life for my sake will find it"? (Matt. 16:25).

Doing the Best You Know How (4:8-9)

Mark Twain is reported to have said that he was not so much disturbed by those things in the Bible that he did not understand as he was by those things he understood but did not do. Doing what we know we ought to do is the theme of Philippians 4:8-9: "Finally, brethren, whatever is true, whatever is honorable, whatever is just, whatever is pure, whatever is lovely, whatever is gracious, if there is any excellence, if there is anything worthy of praise, think about these things. What you have learned and received and heard and seen in me, do; and the God of peace will be with you."

Verse 8 is a list of virtues that were prized by moralists in ancient society. These were qualities that pagan society considered right and good. In other words, Paul was reminding the Christians that they could not ignore the basic building blocks of a good life. Christian morality goes further and probes deeper than these qualities, but it affirms rather than denies these virtues.

Paul said that Christians were to "think about these things." The word translated "think about" means more than thoughtful contemplation; it means to "reflect upon and allow these qualities of living to shape your conduct."[4]

The words of verse 8 thus present a recurring Bible theme: the source of real strength of character is within the mind and heart. We are told, for example, to keep our hearts with all diligence, for out of the heart are the issues of life (Prov. 4:23). Again the Bible says, "As a man thinketh in his heart, so is he" (Prov. 23:7, KJV). Jesus taught that the cause of human defilement is a heart filled with evil thoughts (Mark 7:18-23). In Philippians 4:8 the apostle was summoning his readers to develop the best in attitude and in motive.

But Paul was not willing to make everyday morality the basis for Christian morality. Neither was he content to say only "think about these things." In verse 9 he went beyond verse 8 both in the content and in the response of Christian morality.

As to the content, Paul reminded them of what they had learned from him and what they had seen exemplified in him (see 3:17). Pagan morality, even at its best, provides only a beginning point for

Christians. Paul had taught them and modeled for them the way of life for Christians.

The key word in verse 9 is *do*. They were not only to let right shape their attitudes and convictions, they were to put what is right into practice. Thus verse 9 is a clarion call to put right attitudes into action. One must not only *think* the best; he must also *do* the best. Inspired feelings and good intentions are not enough. When the Lord commends his faithful stewards, he will say not, "Well felt," not "Well intended," but, "Well done."

A Sunday School teacher in a Children's Department asked his group to draw a picture of a good boy. When the young artists were finished, the results were revealing. Most of them had attempted to draw a boy who was not into any mischief. Such a portrait usually depicted a young fellow dressed in his best suit and sitting quietly in a chair. On his face was a look of angelic serenity. One small scholar, however, captured more correctly the Bible's idea of goodness. He drew a Boy Scout helping an old lady across a busy street. What is real goodness anyway? Is it merely refraining from evil? Is it not rather the practice of the best principles of truth and love of which we are capable?

Paul thus called for putting into practice what we know to be right and good. Notice the promise that goes with this: "the God of peace will be with you" (v. 9). In other words, doing the best you know how is one of the clues to the secret of contentment.

Christ-sufficiency, not Self-sufficiency (4:10-13)

Paul himself is our best model of one who had discovered the secret of contentment. His statement of contentment occurs in Philippians 4:10-13, which is a part of Paul's expression of gratitude to the Philippians for their financial help.

Scholars wrestle with this question: "Why did Paul wait so long to thank the Philippians?" Epaphroditus had brought the gift much earlier than Paul's letter, and even in the letter Paul's expression of gratitude comes at the end of the letter.

One possibility is that Paul had already thanked the

Philippians—either in an earlier letter, which we no longer have, or through some oral communication. One reason for this assumption is that Paul was not the kind of person to put off an expression of gratitude and appreciation. Another reason is the manner in which Paul expressed his thanks in 4:10-20.

If this was intended to be primarily an expression of gratitude, it surely ranks as one of the world's most unusual thank-you notes. We often say that it is not the gift but the thought behind it that counts. In essence, this is what Paul said. The apostle was more grateful for the givers than for the gift. He even went so far as to say that he could have gotten along without the gift.

Frank Stagg makes this observation about Paul's approach in 4:10-20: "In these verses Paul walks a chalk line which avoids ingratitude on the one hand and dependence on the other. Positively, he expresses profound gratitude for generous and meaningful gifts and at the same time maintains his independence of external support. His ultimate resources are within himself, these not of himself, but of Christ; and in Christ he has a sufficiency which has a sovereign independence of all circumstance, whether plenty or poverty, whether surrounded by friends or abandoned."[5]

Paul began this final part of his letter by writing: "I rejoice in the Lord greatly that now at length you have revived your concern for me; you were indeed concerned for me, but you had no opportunity" (4:10). The first part of this verse might sound as if Paul were complaining because they had taken so long to revive any interest in helping him. The last part of the verse corrects this possible misunderstanding: they had been concerned all along, but they had not had the opportunity. Perhaps this means that they had lacked the resources to help Paul. Probably it means that they had lost contact with Paul in his missionary travels and adventures, or that they had no way to get aid to him.

Verses 11-13 present the key to Paul's secret of contentment: "Not that I complain of want; for I have learned, in whatever state I am, to be content. I know how to be abased, and I know how to abound; in any and in all circumstances I have learned the secret of facing plenty and hunger, abundance and want. I can do all things in him who strengthens me."

Paul did not deny that he had been in a condition of need, but he did refuse to complain about his needs. In fact he had learned a wonderful secret—the secret of contentment. Whether he had much or little did not alter his basic stance of gratitude and contentment.

Two words in verses 11-12 deserve special attention: The word translated "I have learned the secret" (4:12) is a technical word often used to describe an initiation into one of the Greek mystery religions. These initiations involved the revelation of certain mysteries. Paul said that he had been initiated into the secret of contentment.

The word translated "content" in verse 11 is another technical word. This word was used by the Stoics to describe their understanding of contentment. The word literally means "self-sufficing." The Stoics believed in self-sufficiency. They taught that a person should be so sufficient within himself that he could be indifferent to his circumstances. The Stoic tried to reduce his basic needs to the bare minimum. F. W. Beare tells of the Stoic who observed a child drinking water using only his hands. The Stoic threw away his cup saying, "A child has vanquished me in economy."[6]

Paul claimed to have found the secret of contentment and sufficiency for which the Stoics and all men seek. However, Paul's approach to contentment was profoundly different from the approach of the Stoics. The Stoics taught that the secret of contentment lies in self-sufficiency. A person should banish any desire from his mind. He should learn to accept life as it comes, teaching himself to need nothing and no one but himself.

Verse 13 states Paul's view, "I can do all things in him who strengthens me." Many late manuscripts add *"Christ."* Either way the repetition of "in Christ" throughout the chapter leaves no question who Paul meant when he wrote "in him."

The secret of Paul's contentment was not self-sufficiency, but Christ-sufficiency. If he had said only "I can do all things," that would have been self-sufficiency. Paul made it plain, however, that it was the Lord who strengthened him. He repeatedly denied that he could do all things. In fact he expressly stated that there was no good in his own life apart from God. Paul described life apart from Christ as life in the flesh. In Romans 7:18 he wrote, "I know that nothing good dwells within me, that is, in my flesh." When this verse is contrasted with Philippians 4:13, we clearly see Paul's secret. He was a man in Christ. So far as he was concerned, the man in Christ already has the pearl of great price (see 3:7-8). He also knows the one who strengthens him so that he can face and overcome any danger or privation (see 1:12-26).

It is not surprising that Philippians 4:13 is a favorite verse of so many people. It sums up succinctly and powerfully what so many have discovered is the secret of one of life's most profound mysteries—how to live with peace and joy in the face of life's changing circumstances.

Gratitude and Generosity (4:14-20)

In verses 10-20 Paul moved back and forth between thanking the Philippians for their help and expressing his own sufficiency in Christ apart from their help. Verse 10 expresses thanks; verses 11-13, his sufficiency in Christ. Verses 14-16 return to the theme of Paul's gratitude for their kindness, not only in their more recent help but also in the earlier expressions of their concern: "Yet it was kind of you to share my trouble. And you Philippians yourselves know that in the beginning of the gospel, when I left Macedonia, no church entered into partnership with me in giving and receiving except you only; for even in Thessalonica you sent me help once and again."

After Paul's first visit to Philippi, he had gone to Thessalonica (Acts 17:1-2). More than once during that time the Philippians had sent financial aid to Paul. Paul's Corinthian correspondence shows that although he believed in the right of financial support for a minister, he had deliberately refused to ask for pay from the Corinthians (1 Cor. 9). While he was in Corinth, some of his financial needs were met by brethren from Macedonia, probably from Philippi. In other words, from the very beginning of their relationship Paul had been generously helped by the Philippians. Paul also commended the sacrificial spirit of the churches of Macedonia in their participation in the offering for the poor in the Judean churches (2 Cor. 8:1-5).

The word translated "share" in verse 14 is a verb form of *koinonia* with a prefix meaning "together with." Paul considered the Philippians to be partners in the gospel (see comments on 1:3-8). Their giving was a natural response in such a partnership. They were joined together with Paul in the gospel and in the trouble that came to those who preached it. Thus Paul did not write a thank-you note as if the Philippians had given a gift to him personally; rather he wrote acknowledging their support as further evidence of their partnership in the gospel.

Having stated once again his joy in this partnership (4:14-16), Paul also once again stated his own sufficiency apart from their gift. He wrote, "Not that I seek the gift; but I seek the fruit which increases to your credit" (4:17).

Paul did not deny that the gift he received from Philippi had met a real need. He did, however, make it plain that he was more grateful for the disposition to give on the part of the Philippians than he was for the gift itself. Their giving revealed their likeness to the gracious Giver of every good and perfect gift. It thrilled Paul to see this unmistakable evidence of their nearness to the Lord.

Any appeal for money in the name of the Lord must bear this principle in mind. A church must develop givers, not just raise gifts. Only an uninformed person could not be aware of the fact that it takes money to strive to carry out the Great Commission. But let a church beware seeking the money and losing sight of those who give it.

What did Paul mean by "fruit which increases to your credit" (v. 17)? The Bible teaches that money is part of the transient, temporal order of things. Material things, however, can be invested in the eternal, spiritual affairs of God's kingdom. A man will leave his money behind, but he will carry his stingy disposition or his generous spirit with him. A man will soon be deprived of his possessions, but he will never be separated from those souls helped by his giving. Is this not what the Lord meant by laying up "treasures in heaven"? (Matt. 6:19-21).

Verse 18 repeats and enlarges on the thought in verse 12: "I have received full payment, and more; I am filled, having received from Epaphroditus the gifts you sent, a fragrant offering, a sacrifice acceptable and pleasing to God."

This was Paul's way of repeating the two themes of verses 10-20. On one hand, Paul personally claimed that he had received more than enough to meet his needs. On the other hand, he acknowledged that their gift was not just money sent to Paul but a sacrificial offering to God himself.

Verse 19 is a fitting climax to this passage, "And my God will supply every need of yours according to his riches in glory in Christ Jesus."

In deep gratitude Paul made the inspired promise of verse 19. This verse has sometimes been used as a proof-text for the theory of "giving-in-order-to-get." This is not a Christian doctrine. There is a legitimate doctrine of rewards in the Bible; but the reward is the by-product, not the motive for giving. Believers do not give in order to receive; they give because they have received.

What then does Paul mean? In 2 Corinthians 9:8 he made a similar promise. He said that "God is able to provide you with every blessing in abundance, so that you may always have enough of everything and may provide in abundance for every good work." The word translated "enough" is the noun form of the word translated "content" in Philippians 4:11.

In other words, God makes this promise to a generous giver: "I will give you enough so that you can continue to give to others in a way that matches my giving to you." The key to this promise is the word "enough." As we have seen, the word was not a reference to wealth but to a contentment with what one has. G. R. Beasley-Murray makes this pertinent comment on 2 Corinthians 9:8: "This is spoken to Christian people who understand Christian restraint: *enough* is enough! God does not promise to provide in such fashion that we 'Keep up with the Joneses.' . . . God gives a man *enough* to have contentment in life and to enable him to be rich in good works and generous giving."[7]

Someone once asked a millionaire, "How much money does a man need to have enough?" He replied quickly, "Just a little more." By contrast, Christians who take the New Testament seriously answer the question this way: "A person has enough when he can meet his own basic needs and be able to share generously with those in need." Obviously, the important factor is the secret of contentment as reflected in Philippians 4.

Paul himself is a sterling example of a man whose every need had been supplied out of the wealth of God in Christ Jesus. God had not made Paul a millionaire, but he had blessed him with the gift of contentment. This in turn enabled him to be even more giving, and his joy abounded as he gave more and more of himself for the cause of Christ.

The New Testament plants the doctrine of giving in Christian soil at the foot of the cross, not in the hard ground of the marketplace. If every man who gave generously were assured thereby that he would become wealthy, only a poor businessman would pass up such an opportunity. Shrewd and worldly people would forsake the stock market and the race track, and the church would soon find money-changers once again in the courts of the Lord. True religion is not a way of material gain, but godliness with contentment is still great gain (1 Timothy 6:5-6).

The familiar Christmas story of Ebenezer Scrooge is an illustration of this truth. The miser who thought Christmas was a "humbug" finally learned his lesson. He set out, therefore, to outdo everyone in the spirit of giving. What was his reward? He was already a wealthy man, and his riches had not brought him happiness. Was his reward not the joy he received in giving? He sought and expected no refund for what he gave away. Scrooge was no doubt somewhat less wealthy in terms of pounds and shillings because of what he gave away. But he was never more truly rich in all his life! He had finally learned that it is more blessed to give than to receive.

The tremendous promise of verse 19 moved Paul to a doxology: "To our God and Father be glory for ever and ever. Amen" (4:20). Then he closed with a brief word of parting, such as was typical of ancient letters: "Greet every saint in Christ Jesus. The brethren who are with me greet you. All the saints greet you, especially those of Caesar's household" (4:21-22; see comments on 1:1-8,12-18).

Without losing any of his spiritual momentum Paul moved from one amen to another. His words of parting are climaxed by a benediction prayer. The apostle would be in Philippi if he could, but he reminded the Christians that there was one at their sides better equipped than he to help them. He trusted the God of grace to be with them: "The grace of the Lord Jesus Christ be with your spirit" (4:23).

Notes

Chapter 1

[1]Frank Stagg, *The Broadman Bible Commentary*, Vol. 11 (Nashville: Broadman Press, 1971), p. 185.

[2]J. B. Lightfoot, *St. Paul's Epistle to the Philippians* (A Revised Text: Grand Rapids, Michigan: Zondervan Publishing House, 1913, 1953), pp. 181-269.

[3]Ralph P. Martin, *Philippians* in the *New Century Bible* (London: Marshall, Morgan and Scott, 1976), p. 56.

Chapter 2

[1]Jerry Leiber, "Is That All There Is?" (New York: Yellow Dog Music, Inc., 1969).

[2]From *The New English Bible, New Testament*, Second Edition. © The Delegates of the Oxford University Press, and the Syndics of the Cambridge University Press, 1961, 1970. Reprinted by permission.

[3]Emil Brunner, *Eternal Hope*, translated by Harold Knight (Philadelphia: The Westminster Press, 1954), p. 152.

[4]Oscar Cullmann, *Christ and Time*, translated by Floyd V. Filson (Philadelphia: The Westminster Press, 1950), p. 240.

[5]Robert J. Dean, *God's Big Little Words* (Nashville: Broadman Press, 1975), p. 76.

[6]F. B. Meyer, *The Epistle to the Philippians* (London: Marshall, Morgan and Scott, 1952), pp. 39-40.

[7]Jesse C. Fletcher, *Bill Wallace of China* (Nashville, Tennessee: Broadman Press, 1963), p. 151.

Chapter 3

[1]Marvin R. Vincent, *The Epistles to the Philippians and to Philemon* ("International Critical Commentary"; Edinburgh: T. and T. Clark, 1955), p. 32.

[2]J. B. Lightfoot, *Saint Paul's Epistle to the Philippians* (A Revised Text; Grand Rapids, Michigan: Zondervan Publishing House, 1953), p. 106.

[3]Martin, *op. cit.*, p. 81.

[4]From *The Bible in Today's English Version*. Old Testament: Copyright © American Bible Society, 1976. New Testament, 1966, 1971, 1976. Used by permission. Subsequent quotations are marked (TEV).

[5]Ulysses S. Grant, *Personal Memoirs of U. S. Grant* (New York: Charles L. Webster and Company, 1885), I, p. 365.

[6]Vincent, *op. cit.*, p. 53.

[7]Albert D. Belden, *George Whitefield-The Awakener* (Nashville: Cokesbury Press, 1930), p. 234.

Chapter 4

[1]Grand Rapids, Michigan: Zondervan Publishing House, 1974.

[2]Martin, p. 102.

[3]Vincent, p. 57.

[4]R. C. H. Lenski, *The Interpretation of St. Paul's Epistles to the Galatians, to the Ephesians, and to the Philippians* (Columbus, Ohio: The Wartburg Press, 1946), p. 770.

[5]F. W. Beare, *A Commentary on the Epistle to the Philippians* (New York: Harper and Row, Publishers, 1959), p. 86.

[6]Stagg, p. 197.

Chapter 5

[1]W. L. White, *They Were Expendable* (New York: Harcourt, Brace and Company, 1942).

[2]Charles E. Maddry, *Christ's Expendables* (Nashville, Tennessee: Broadman Press, 1947).

[3]See comments on 3:20-21; cf. A. M. Hunter, *The Gospel According to St. Paul* (Philadelphia: The Westminster Press, 1966), pp. 14-57.

[4]Beare, p. 90.

[5]Lightfoot, p. 119.

[6]Martin, p. 108.

[7]George Seaver, *David Livingstone: His Life and Letters* (New York: Harper and Brothers Publishers, 1957), p. 632.

[8]Vincent, p. 78.

[9]E. F. Scott, "The Apostle to the Philippians," *The Interpreter's Bible*, Vol. 11 (Nashville: Abingdon Press, 1955), p. 71.

[10]Stagg, p. 202.

[11]Charles Kingsley, *Hypatia* (New York: Rand, McNally and Company, n.d.), p. 67.

Chapter 6

[1]William James, *The Varieties of Religious Experience* (New York: Longmans, Green and Co., 1902, 1928), p. 189.

[2]William Barclay, *Turning to God: a Study of Conversion in the Book of Acts and Today* (Philadelphia: The Westminster Press, 1964), p. 25.

[3]Beare, p. 100.

[4]Scott, p. 72.

[5]*Ibid.*

[6]Stagg, p. 203.

[7]Scott, p. 80.

[8]Barclay, p. 42.

[9]Vincent, p. 99.

[10]Stagg, p. 206.

[11]Clovis G. Chappell, *Men That Count* (New York: Richard R. Smith, Inc., 1929), p. 3.

[12]Barclay, p. 28.

Chapter 7

[1]Vincent, p. 110.

[2]Martin, p. 139.

[3]Gerald Kennedy, *The Parables* (New York: Harper and Brothers, Publishers, 1960), p. 46.

[4]Stagg, pp. 208-209.

[5]Scott, p. 92.

[6]Martin, p. 141.

[7]Stagg, p. 210.

[8]Walter Schmithals, *Gnosticism in Corinth: an Investigation of the Letters to the Corinthians*, translated by John E. Steely (Nashville: Abingdon Press, 1971), pp. 218-231.

[9]Stagg, pp. 209-210.